sushi rice

lamb and vegetable couscous

baked sea bass with polenta triangles

sweet tomato chutney

crespelle with ricotta and spinach

chocolate-wrapped hazelnut cake

MASTER CHEFS COOK

kosher

All the recipes in *Master Chefs Cook Kosher* are kosher. However, Chronicle Books regrets that some are mislabeled and apologizes for the following corrections:

❦

The following recipes should be labeled *Dairy:* Pistachio Lace Cookies, page 30; Baked Sea Bass with Polenta Triangles, page 52; Sautéed Shiitake Mushrooms, page 59. ❦ Please also note that the following recipes use Pareve Chicken Stock, which is on page 168, not the Chicken Stock on page 167: Mushroom and Hazelnut Soup, page 18; Luciano's Two-in-One Risotto, page 53; Pumpkin–White Bean Chowder, page 72; Goat Cheese–Almond Chiles Rellenos (using Almond Sauce), pages 73 and 74; Roasted Eggplant Soup, page 105. ❦ For Passover, omit the flour and the mustard in the Marinated Whitefish with Pine Nuts on page 38. ❦ Since kosher Parmigiano-Reggiano may be difficult to find, we suggest that you use kosher Parmesan for the Mushroom Salad and the Crunchy Fennel Salad on page 42 and the Conchiglie with Mushrooms and Radicchio on page 43.

MASTER CHEFS COOK

kosher

CHRONICLE BOOKS
SAN FRANCISCO

by judy zeidler
photographs by michael lamotte

Library of Congress Cataloging-in-Publication Data:
Zeidler, Judy.
    Master chefs cook kosher / by Judy Zeidler;
    photographs by Michael Lamotte.
       176 p. 21 x 23.5 cm
       Includes index.
       ISBN 0-8118-1402-5
       1. Cookery, Jewish. 2. Kosher food. 3. Cookery,
International. I. Title.
       TX724.Z454 1998
       641.5'676–dc21   97-30795
                             CIP

Printed in Hong Kong

Designed by Melissa Passehl Design

Designer's Assistant Charlotte Lambrechts

Photographer's Assistant Bill Checkvala

Food Styling by Sandra Cook

Food Stylist's Assistant Allyson Levy

Prop Styling by Sara Slavin

The photographer would like to thank Fillamento, San Francisco, for their props.

Distributed in Canada by:
Raincoast Books
8680 Cambie Street, Vancouver, B.C. V6P 6M9

10 9 8 7 6 5 4 3 2 1

Chronicle Books
85 Second Street, San Francisco, CA 94105

Web Site: www.chronbooks.com

MASTER CHEFS COOK KOSHER
table of contents

ACKNOWLEDGMENTS

To my terrific husband, Marvin, for his encouragement and patience in reading and re-reading this book. And for the fun we've had cooking kosher together for so many years. My kindest critics, all wonderful children and grandchildren. My agent, Fred Hill, for his continuous support. The group at Chronicle Books, Bill LeBlond, Leslie Jonath, Sarah Putman, and Susan Derecskey, for liking my idea and going with this concept. The Jewish Television Network, which helped me create Judy's Kitchen, and especially Alan Block, Jay Sanderson, and Harvey Leher. My testers Sue Cheldin, Tracy Flatow, Shirley and Lud Renick, and Florine Sikking. A special thank-you to Carolee Blumin, for her perfection in testing and recording notes, as well as her photographs of all the dishes. To my tireless friend Joan Bram, who is always available for extra duty as a tester and taster! Special thanks to Sara J. Mitchell, for her skillful attention to details like spelling and syntax, and for prodding me to do my best work. And to Janice Wald Henderson, for her excellent editing.

I THOUGHT I HAD DONE every kind of kosher-cooking project imaginable —lectures, cooking classes, and writing cookbooks and newspaper and magazine articles. I had also appeared as a guest on local and national television and radio shows. But when the Jewish Television Network offered me a weekly thirty-minute show, I was very excited and also a little anxious. 🌿 Thirty minutes felt like a long time to cook for a television audience. I started to worry: Would I run out of ideas? What if the conversation came to a halt? Suppose I spilled hot soup on myself? Perhaps I'd have a guest chef who doesn't speak English well? Finally, I cast my fears and doubts aside and said, "Yes, I will do the show!" I called it *Judy's Kitchen.* 🌿 The first show was filmed in my own kosher kitchen, with one camera and a crew of three. It has been a huge success ever since. If fan mail means anything, *Judy's Kitchen* is one of the network's most popular programs. 🌿 After doing so many shows, I wrote this book because many food lovers who keep kosher feel frustrated. They read about exciting new restaurants, about brilliant young chefs and their creative recipes, but they can't prepare the dishes because they're not in keeping with dietary laws. This book comes to the rescue by adapting innovative recipes for the kosher kitchen. 🌿 Here you will find the best recipes we ever cooked on *Judy's Kitchen.* Most are fairly simple, since we were limited by time. All prove that you can observe kosher dietary rules and still achieve delicious, sophisticated results far beyond the usual latkes, gefilte fish, chicken soup, and brisket. 🌿 The recipes are virtually foolproof; they've been prepared on camera and tasted by the television crews, who lined up for samples. Then they were tested and retested by my capable staff. Hundreds of viewers have written me to offer words of encouragement and request the recipes. They loved these dishes, and you will, too. 🌿 I invite you to step into *Judy's Kitchen* and meet some talented chefs. And enjoy their fabulous recipes. 🌿 Judy Zeidler, Los Angeles, California, 1997

How *JUDY'S KITCHEN* began is simple. Through my interest in food and travel and my role as a restaurateur, I have met many famous chefs. Some have become close personal friends. When I invited them to appear on my new show, they accepted with delight. ❧ Most of the chefs knew little about kosher cooking. They knew that Jews don't eat pork, but they didn't know that some other meats or cuts of meat were forbidden. They were not aware that poultry must be specially treated, that shellfish is taboo, that meat may not be served with dairy products. But they learned fast and enjoyed the challenge. ❧ Translating the ethnic cuisines of many chefs to kosher, including French, Irish, Asian, Italian, Moroccan, and Indian, as well as American home-style cooking, was not difficult. My guest chefs admitted that nothing was lost in the translation. ❧ Before their appearances on my show, we'd talk on the telephone and plan the menus. I reminded them that we'd have to adapt the recipes for a kosher kitchen. They would fax me ideas and I'd approve them, keeping in mind how interesting each dish would be from a teaching standpoint, as well as its appeal to viewers. Timing and necessary equipment were also considerations. After laying the groundwork, we'd set a date for the shoot. ❧ When the chefs first arrived on the set, we'd talk about new restaurants, recipes, and cookbooks—typical food talk that helped them relax. ❧ As the cameras began to roll, I would welcome the viewers to *Judy's Kitchen* and introduce the guest chef. I then gave the audience a little background information, and we discussed the menu and/or recipes we would prepare. When one dish was finished, we'd take a break and get ready for the show's second half. ❧ Often we found time for a third dish. Finally, we presented all the dishes and discussed ideas on how to enhance the recipes, add attractive garnishes, and use the dishes in appealing menus. I then interviewed my guest about his or her future projects. Some chefs were contemplating writing a cookbook, opening a new restaurant, getting married, even having a baby—one was about to become a father of twins. ❦ Exhausted, but thrilled about how well the show went and the anticipation of its airing, we said good-bye and thank-you to the chef and crew. Most chefs were so delighted with their appearance that they ended the show by saying, "When can we do this again?" For me, the early morning taping was not the end, because we usually shot two shows in one day. Before I had time to realize how tired I was, it was time to greet my next guest with smiling enthusiasm. ❦ Of course, every episode didn't always go smoothly. I remember some bumps, which didn't seem funny at the time but make me smile now. ❦ In the early days of *Judy's Kitchen*, with one camera and a low budget, we often ran into trouble. Once, a wiring problem in the sound projector made it necessary for a technician to work directly under a counter where I was rolling out pasta. In a short time, I sprinkled her head with so much flour that her hair turned prematurely white. It was hard to keep from laughing whenever I caught a glimpse of her. ❦ Pierre Pelech, chef-manager of the Hotel Alizea on Saint Martin Island in the French West Indies, mistakenly put half a cup of salt instead of sugar into his swiss chard tart. Of course it was inedible, but no one had a clue until the end of the segment, when Pierre confessed his error off camera. The crew, who loved sampling the recipes, were disappointed, so after the show, the chef quickly made another tart for the crew. ❦ French chef Michel Richard, chef-owner of Citrus Restaurant in Los Angeles and Citronelle in Washington, D.C., and Santa Barbara, had a major mishap when pouring duck and sauce from a very large pot into a large strainer. The duck and sauce fell into the strainer at the same time, splashing sauce all over, including on me. Michel was afraid to survey the damage—he kept his head bent over the huge pot on the stove—while I tried to signal him that I was okay. The sauce just added a little color to my hands-on approach to cooking. ❦ In the middle of shooting a show in my home kitchen, the Brentwood

Fire Department arrived, rushed in, and demanded to see our permit. Of course, we didn't have one. They wanted to close the set immediately, but we pleaded for fifteen minutes to complete the show. Although their stern faces made us nervous, we continued to bake the biscotti, which turned out fine. (You can be sure we got a permit for our next show.) ❦ One day we were shooting the show in Michel Richard's luxurious kitchen at home. One of the camera crew fell off his stool with a loud thud. It seemed he was suffering from sleep deprivation and was playing catch-up during the show. After he gulped down two cups of coffee, we reshot the entire segment. Today we have more cameras, a larger crew, and lots of technical improvements, but I really miss those early days when anything could happen—and it usually did! ❦ When we were working on the Mary Bergin Passover cake show, we had to chill the cake so it would stay firm but still have it close by to present on camera. We filled a large bowl with crushed ice but neglected to place the cake on the ice. Mary didn't remember that the cake was not there, but fortunately I did—just in time. I ad-libbed, "We'll be right back with the cake." The segment was saved and the cake looked fabulous. ❦ Michael Franks found aïoli a little tricky to make on live TV. When he looked into the food processor after all the ingredients were mixed together, he faced a strange-looking liquid. But the show must go on! So he kept it a secret; later he made a new and perfect version to accompany his delicious fried gefilte fish. ❦ Patrick Healy couldn't prepare the veal shanks in advance and it takes over two hours to cook them. Since we had only thirty minutes, I watched Patrick prepare one veal shank in record time to present at the conclusion of the show. Fortunately, it looked as if it was cooked through. ❦ When the segment with Michel Richard and Roger Vergé began, Michel decided to give me a French lesson on camera. I thought he was serious and that we would have to do a retake, but he was just joking. Instead of an embarrassing moment, it turned out to be an amusing introduction.

A Simple Guide to Kosher Cooking

Although kosher laws may seem complicated at first, they actually follow an understandable logic. For starters, the word kosher *means "fit" or "proper" and describes the foods that the Old Testament declares appropriate to consume. Kosher foods are divided into three classifications: meat, dairy, and pareve. Meat must never be consumed with dairy, but pareve foods can be eaten with either meat or dairy.*

meat: Only animals that chew cud and have a cloven hoof may be eaten, so the consumption of pork is forbidden, as are birds of prey and scavenger birds.

For meat and poultry to be deemed kosher, the animals must be slaughtered under ritualistic rabbinical guidelines. Kosher Jews consider such butchering the most humane.

After meat or poultry is purchased from a kosher butcher, any remaining blood must be removed through a process called kashering. (In the Bible, blood is regarded as the life of the flesh and must be removed before an animal is eaten.) Meat is soaked in cold water for half an hour, rinsed, and sprinkled with coarse salt for one hour before a second rinse. Broiled meats are excluded from the kashering process, since broiling allows the free flow of blood. Since liver contains much blood, it must always be broiled.

dairy: The obvious foods in this group are milk and milk products such as cheese, cream, yogurt, and ice cream.

pareve: Pareve (pronounced PAR-eve) includes foods that are not meat or dairy. All fresh fruits and vegetables and grains are pareve and can be served with either dairy or meat dishes.

Fish falls into the pareve category. It's considered an important component of a kosher diet. Only fish with fins and scales, such as cod, whitefish, salmon, and trout are acceptable. Shellfish, catfish, monkfish, and eel are among the fish that are not. Despite the fact that fish have blood, no special kashering process is needed.

Keeping a Kosher Kitchen

In order to keep kosher, it's necessary to have at least two sets of dishes and utensils since meat and milk products can never be prepared in the same pots or served on the same plates. (Kosher cooks even use different soap for washing each set.) Kosher households must also have an additional set of dishes and utensils that are used only for Passover.

DAIRY AND FISH MENUS

part one

CONTEMPORARY chefs love to cook with fish and dairy products, so it's not surprising that this section overflows with innovative menus. French, Italian, Mexican, American—they're all here and they're all kosher. Best of all, they're all delicious. I ought to know: I've tasted every one of them. ❦ My parents often fed me dairy dinners when I was young, and that usually meant cheese blintzes and salmon latkes. This book offers some new ways to go dairy: For example, Josie Le Balch's Italian crepes with ricotta and spinach are a welcome change from the traditional blintzes. And Joyce Goldstein's salmon croquettes could be considered an update on salmon latkes, especially since they're jazzed up with aïoli. ❦ My mother always baked fish in the traditional Jewish fashion, at low heat for more than one hour, until it turned soft and mushy—oy vay! I always marvel when I taste Angelo Auriano's moist and flaky sea bass, roasted for only ten minutes in a high-heat oven. Those of you who grew up with moms who baked pasta with tomato sauce until the noodles turned dry and hard will find Johanne Killeen and George Germon's quickly prepared pastas simply glorious. ❦ I've created a couple of mix-and-match menus for this chapter to speed you on the way to developing your own. ❦ A SALMON SPECTACULAR : *Goat Cheese and Tomato Appetizer, Mushroom and Hazelnut Soup, Grilled Salmon with Baby Vegetables and Tomato Concassé, Michel's Chocolate Sorbet, and Pistachio Lace Cookies.* This may appear to be an ambitious menu, but the appetizer and soup can be prepared at least a day in advance, as well as the sorbet and cookies. The salmon is the only last-minute preparation. ❦ AN INSPIRED ITALIAN MEAL : *Radicchio-Orange Salad or Crunchy Fennel Salad, Baked Sea Bass with Polenta Triangles, Mascarpone Custard with Fruits of the Season, and Pasticcini alle Nocciole (Hazelnut Cookies)*

JOYCE GOLDSTEIN
mediterranean food maven

about the chef: Joyce Goldstein showcased Mediterranean cuisine long before it became popular throughout the country. She was chef of the casual café at Berkeley's Chez Panisse, where she learned the restaurant business firsthand in the course of three years. Joyce founded the California Street Cooking School, which began in an old storefront building a few blocks from her home in San Francisco. She also taught kitchen design at the University of California and has written several cookbooks, including *The Mediterranean Kitchen*.

When Joyce opened Square One restaurant, San Francisco took notice. Her energy and creativity mesmerized the city. Joyce says that she named her restaurant Square One because every day they start out with a new menu and fresh ingredients. Joyce was one of the first superstar chefs to serve Passover menus. They were hardly the norm: One featured Italian-Jewish cuisine, another offered Sephardic dishes.

In 1993, Joyce won the James Beard Perrier-Jouët Award for Best Chef in California. Joyce recently closed Square One to concentrate on food consulting. She is on the board of several charities, including Meals on Wheels and Open Hand, and donates much of her time to community affairs. Not surprisingly, both her son and daughter have followed in her footsteps.

on judy's kitchen: Unlike many chefs who appear on television flying by the seat of their pants, Joyce came well prepared. She brought notes, neatly typed recipes, and some new ideas. A no-nonsense guest and a true professional, Joyce was able to explain her excellent recipes clearly and concisely, giving viewers enough confidence to duplicate the dishes at home.

Before rushing off to catch her flight to San Francisco, Joyce and I had a chance to relax and chat. She said how happy she was to have had an opportunity to cook kosher with me. We also discussed her new cookbook, *Cucina Ebraica*, and how she had had the desire to write an Italian-Jewish cookbook for a long time, and that it was finished at last.

menu

~ Mushroom and Hazelnut Soup

~ Potato Strudel

~ Salmon Croquettes, Jewish Style with Aïoli

When onions are cooked slowly, they become very sweet and add fine flavor to a dish. The classic French onion soup is a perfect example. In this recipe, hazelnuts and mushrooms are combined with the onions for a soup with a remarkably earthy depth of flavor.

1   cup hazelnuts, toasted and peeled (see page 165)

4   tablespoons (½ stick) unsalted butter

6   cups sliced onions (1½ pounds)

2   pounds white or brown mushrooms, cleaned and cut into chunks if large

5   cups hot Chicken Stock (page 167)

1   teaspoon salt

¼   teaspoon freshly ground black pepper

¼   cup chopped parsley or ½ cup sour cream, for garnish

Place the nuts in a food processor and grind until finely chopped. Set aside.

Melt the butter in a large saucepan over medium heat. Add the onions and cook, stirring occasionally, until tender, about 10 minutes. Add the mushrooms and cook, covered, for 5 minutes. Add enough stock to barely cover and bring to a boil. Reduce the heat and simmer for 10 to 15 minutes, or until the mushrooms are soft. Working in batches, puree the mushrooms and onions with the nuts in a food processor or blender, adding a little of the stock. Thin the soup to the desired consistency with stock. Season with salt and pepper. Return the soup to the saucepan and reheat.

To serve, ladle into heated soup bowls and garnish with parsley or sour cream.

Serves 8   Dairy

Garnished with sour cream and chives, this strudel can be served as a first course. It is perfect for your Shavuoth menu.

6   large russet potatoes

3   tablespoons unsalted butter

1   large onion, diced

1   cup ricotta cheese

1   large egg

2   tablespoons minced parsley

2   teaspoons salt, or to taste

1   teaspoon freshly ground black pepper

Pinch of grated nutmeg

12 sheets phyllo dough

8   tablespoons (1 stick) unsalted butter, melted

1   cup sour cream, for garnish (optional)

¼   cup chopped chives, for garnish (optional)

Preheat the oven to 450°F.

Wash the potatoes well and pierce in several places with a fork. Bake for about 1 hour, or until tender. Turn off the oven. Set the potatoes aside until cool enough to handle, then cut lengthwise in half and scoop out the pulp. Put the pulp through a potato ricer, or mash in a mixing bowl.

Melt 3 tablespoons of the butter in a large skillet over medium heat. Add the onion and cook, stirring occasionally, for 10 minutes, or until soft. Add to the potatoes. Add the cheese, egg, parsley, salt, pepper, and nutmeg. Blend well. Let cool. (Filling can be prepared 1 day in advance and refrigerated.)

Lay a sheet of phyllo on a work surface with 1 long side facing you and brush with melted butter. Lay a second sheet on top and brush with melted butter. Repeat with 4 more sheets. Keep unused phyllo covered with wax paper and a damp towel.

Shape half of the potato mixture into a 2-inch-thick log along 1 side of the phyllo, leaving a 2-inch border. Fold in the sides of the phyllo and roll up the strudel, brushing with butter as you roll. Line a baking sheet with foil and brush the foil with melted butter. Place the strudel, seam side down, on the prepared baking sheet. Repeat with the remaining phyllo dough and potato mixture. (The strudels may be wrapped in foil and refrigerated for up to 2 days or frozen.)

Preheat the oven to 400°F.

Bake the strudels for 25 to 30 minutes, or until golden brown. Let rest for 2 to 3 minutes, then cut into thick slices with a serrated knife. Serve garnished with sour cream and chives, if desired.

Serves 8   Dairy

salmon croquettes, jewish style with aïoli

Joyce discovered this recipe in an old Italian-Jewish cookbook that used sweet spices with fish. She served it at her restaurant instead of gefilte fish for Passover, replacing the bread crumbs with matzo meal.

Salmon latkes were a menu staple for my mother. And when our children were growing up, my husband's mother, Gramma Gene, made them often as a special treat when the grandchildren came for lunch. In those days she used canned pink salmon. I like Joyce's upscale version much better (but don't tell anyone).

2	pounds salmon fillet
4	tablespoons (½ stick) unsalted butter
2	cups finely diced onions
1	teaspoon ground cinnamon
¼	teaspoon ground cloves
¼	teaspoon freshly grated nutmeg
¼	cup chopped parsley
1	cup fresh bread crumbs
¾	cup mayonnaise

Salt and freshly ground black pepper, to taste

| 1 | cup dried bread crumbs |
| 1 | cup clarified butter (see page 165) or olive oil, for frying |

Aïoli (recipe follows)

Lemon wedges, for garnish

Poach or steam the salmon for about 8 minutes, or until flaky and cooked through but not dry. Let cool. Flake the fish into small pieces with your fingers, removing any bones.

Melt the butter in a medium skillet over medium heat. Add the onions and cook until tender, but not brown, about 5 minutes. Stir in the spices and parsley and cook for 1 to 2 minutes longer. Combine the onion mixture, salmon, fresh bread crumbs, and mayonnaise. Season with salt and pepper.

Shape the salmon mixture into 12 to 16 patties, about 1 inch thick. Coat on all sides with the dried bread crumbs. Cover with plastic wrap and place on a baking sheet lined with parchment or wax paper. (Croquettes may be refrigerated at this point for up to 6 hours.)

To cook the croquettes, heat the clarified butter or olive oil in 2 large skillets over medium heat. Add the croquettes and sauté until golden on all sides, 6 to 8 minutes.

To serve, arrange salmon croquettes on plates, spoon Aïoli on the side, and garnish with lemon wedges.

Serves 6 to 8   Dairy

aïoli (garlic mayonnaise)

2   egg yolks, at room temperature (see Note)

1   tablespoon fresh lemon juice, or more to taste

2   cups olive oil

1   tablespoon garlic mashed with a pinch of salt

3   tablespoons fresh orange juice

2   tablespoons grated orange zest

2   teaspoons freshly ground black pepper

Salt, to taste

Whisk the egg yolks and lemon juice in a food processor or mixing bowl until blended. Gradually whisk or beat in the oil. The mixture should be thick and emulsified. Whisk or beat in the garlic, orange juice, orange zest, and pepper. Season with salt. Cover with plastic wrap and refrigerate until ready to serve. (Aïoli will keep refrigerated for 2 to 3 days.)

Makes 2½ to 3 cups   Pareve

Note: Since raw egg yolks may contain salmonella, you may choose to omit this recipe and replace it with 2 cups of commercial mayonnaise and 1 mashed garlic clove.

about the chef: Many French chefs have volatile personalties, but not Pierre Pelech. This unassuming chef is a charmer. His quiet demeanor doesn't mean, however, that his food is timid. His flavors are bright and fresh, with an abundance of Provençal verve. A Holocaust survivor, he was hidden during the war by a family on a farm in France.

Pierre attended cooking school in Toulouse, France, and worked at such south of France landmarks as La Réserve in Beaulieu-sur-Mer, Hôtel Metropole in Monte Carlo, and Pavillon Eden Roc at the Cap d'Antibes. It was there that Pierre met Huntington Hartford. Pierre was wooed to America to become Hartford's personal chef. He cooked on Hartford's privately owned Island, Paradise Island, in Nassau, The Bahamas. He also worked in New York and in the Hawaiian Islands, on Maui, Oahu, and Kauai. He then went to Los Angeles to become chef of the highly regarded L'Auberge restaurant for three years.

Pierre staked out a place for himself in Los Angeles at the historic Los Feliz Inn for some twenty-two years. Today he lives where many would call paradise—the French West Indies—with his wife and two daughters. He manages the Hotel Alizea, a small private hotel and restaurant on the island of Saint Martin.

on judy's kitchen: Pierre and I were friends for many years before he appeared on my show. He prepared a menu well suited for any occasion but especially exemplary for breaking the fast on Yom Kippur. Pierre is Jewish, and he remembers that when he was a child, his mother would always welcome the family when they returned from synagogue to break the fast with hot fresh mint tea and sweets before dinner.

When preparing his Tourte de Blette, a tart with a sweet-and-savory Swiss chard filling, Pierre explained that many French families grew their own vegetables and sought ways to use them in every dish, from appetizers to desserts. The Swiss chard in the tarts we prepared on camera were picked by Pierre. They went directly from Judy's garden to *Judy's Kitchen*.

menu

~ Tomato Soup with Fresh Herbes de Provence

~ Roasted Sea Bass with Eggplant and Tomatoes

~ Tourte de Blette (Sweet and Savory Chard Tart)

tomato soup with fresh herbes de provence

This soup, chock-full of fresh vegetables and herbs, tastes like a summer day in Provence. Pierre calls it "sunshine." The soup is thick without any flour, cornstarch, or cream. It's equally delicious served hot or cold. You may want to double the recipe and use the leftovers as a sauce for pasta, fish, or vegetables.

Herbes de Provence:

2   bay leaves

4   sprigs thyme

4   sprigs rosemary

2   sprigs basil

2   tablespoons olive oil

1   medium onion, thinly sliced

1   carrot, thinly sliced

2   stalks celery, thinly sliced

4   garlic cloves, crushed

2   sprigs parsley

4   large tomatoes, diced

3   tablespoons tomato paste

3   cups boiling water

Salt and freshly ground black pepper, to taste

½   cup sour cream, for garnish

6   to 8 small basil leaves, for garnish

To make the Herbes de Provence, cut a large piece of cheesecloth and arrange the herbs in the center. Bring the corners together and tie tightly with string.

Heat the olive oil in a large saucepan over medium heat and sauté the onion, carrot, celery, garlic, and parsley for 5 minutes. Add the tomatoes, tomato paste, and herb bag. Sauté until the tomatoes are heated through and have given off their juice. Add the water, bring to a boil, and simmer for 30 minutes. Remove the herb bag. Lift or strain the vegetables out of the soup and transfer in 3 or 4 batches to a food processor or blender. Puree the vegetables with a small amount of soup with each batch. Return to the soup. Season with salt and pepper. Add additional boiling water, if needed, to thin the soup. Reheat if necessary.

To serve, ladle soup into individual soup bowls. Top each bowl with a dollop of sour cream and a basil leaf.

Serves 6 to 8   Dairy

roasted sea bass with eggplant and tomatoes

Perfect for a Yom Kippur break-the-fast, this roasted fish can be readied for the oven in the morning, covered with plastic wrap, refrigerated, and baked just before serving. It is excellent with steamed rice. Or bake it in advance and serve it chilled with a green salad.

1   sea bass fillet (2 pounds), 1 inch thick

2   large garlic cloves, thinly sliced

½   cup dry white wine

½   cup Vegetable Stock (page 166)

Salt and freshly ground black pepper, to taste

2   tablespoons olive oil

1   large onion, thinly sliced

2   medium tomatoes, thickly sliced

1   small eggplant, thickly sliced

4   sprigs rosemary

4   sprigs thyme

2   bay leaves

8   basil leaves

Preheat the oven to 350°F.

Arrange the sea bass fillet in the center of a baking pan just large enough to hold the fish. With the point of a sharp knife, make several slits in the top of the fillet. Insert a slice of garlic into each slit. Pour the wine and stock over the fish and season generously with salt and pepper.

Heat the oil in a small nonstick skillet over medium heat and sauté the onion slices until they begin to caramelize, about 5 minutes. Arrange them on top of the sea bass. Put the sliced tomatoes and eggplant in the skillet and sauté until lightly browned and soft. Arrange the tomato and eggplant slices alternately over the fish, overlapping slightly. Arrange the rosemary, thyme, bay leaves, and basil on top. Bake until the fish is white and flaky, about 25 minutes.

To serve, slice the sea bass and arrange on individual plates with tomato and eggplant slices on the side. Spoon the pan juices over the fish.

Serves 6 to 8   Pareve

tourte de blette (sweet and savory chard tart)

Blette means chard in French. Most people are surprised that this Niçoise pastry is served as dessert, but when they learn that the chard is combined with raisins, apples, and sugar, and baked in a sweet crust, they are less confused.

This tart was definitely one of the outstanding recipes prepared on Judy's Kitchen, and it has become a favorite in our home to serve to family and friends. For added color and tartness, I occasionally replace the raisins with dried cranberries.

1   unbaked Sweet Pie Crust (recipe follows)

1½ pounds young Swiss chard

3   tart green apples such as Pippin, peeled, cored, and thinly sliced

Juice of 1 lemon

½   cup raisins, soaked in 1 cup rum

2   eggs

1   cup (firmly packed) brown sugar

1   cup pine nuts

2   tablespoons cognac or marc

1   tablespoon olive oil

1   cup grated Parmesan

½   teaspoon salt

Freshly ground black pepper, to taste

Granulated sugar, for garnish

Prepare the pie crust dough and refrigerate it.

Cut out the rib in the center of each chard leaf. Stack the leaves and tightly roll the long way, like a cigar. Cut into thin slices. Wash until the water is clear, and dry with paper towels. (You should have 3 cups, tightly packed, julienned chard.)

Put the apples in a medium bowl, add the lemon juice, and toss to coat the slices. Set aside.

Drain the raisins, reserving the rum for another use. Mix the raisins, eggs, brown sugar, pine nuts, cognac, olive oil, Parmesan, salt, and pepper in a large bowl. Add the chard and mix well.

Preheat the oven to 350°F.

Roll out half of the dough and line a 10-inch pie pan. Spoon the chard mixture, with some of the juice, into the pie shell. Arrange the sliced apples in a circular pattern on top. Roll out the remaining dough and place it over the apples. Press the edges of the top and bottom crusts together gently to seal and trim the edges. Prick the top crust with a fork in several places. Bake for 45 minutes, or until golden brown. Let cool on a rack.

Serve at room temperature. Just before serving, sprinkle with sugar.

Serves 8 to 10   Dairy

sweet pie crust

2   cups unbleached all-purpose flour

¼   cup sugar

Pinch of salt

8   tablespoons (1 stick) unsalted butter, softened and cut into pieces

1   egg, lightly beaten

3   tablespoons cold water

Combine the flour, sugar, salt, and butter in the bowl of an electric mixer. Blend together until the mixture is the consistency of corn-meal. Add the egg and water and mix until the dough comes together. Do not overmix. Shape the dough into a ball, cover with plastic wrap, and refrigerate for 1 hour.

Divide the dough in half. Roll out half of the dough about ¼ inch thick on a large sheet of floured wax paper, forming a circle large enough to line a 10-inch pie dish with a 1½- to 2-inch overhang. Carefully place in the bottom and up the sides of the dish. Fill the pie shell. Roll out

the second half of the dough, cover the filling, crimp, and prick. Bake as directed.

Makes a 10-inch double-crust pie   Dairy

chef's secrets

❧ If you're growing fresh herbs in your garden, always cut them in the morning even for the evening meal. They are more flavorful before the sun dries them out.

❧ To bring out all the flavors in vegetables, always sauté them in very hot oil.

❧ To keep apples from discoloring after peeling, place them in lemon juice. The lemon juice also acts as a flavoring agent.

❧ To select the freshest whole fish, look for shiny scales.

ROGER VERGÉ AND MICHEL RICHARD

french friends cook together

about the chefs: Michel Richard, a close friend, has often cooked on *Judy's Kitchen*. Usually he appears alone (see page 99), but on this occasion, he joined forces with Roger Vergé. Roger, who is based in the south of France, did the appetizer and main course; Michel, who is from Brittany but has restaurants on both the East and West Coasts of the U.S., did the desserts. The chemistry between them was remarkable.

Few chefs are as internationally celebrated as Roger Vergé. He rocketed to stardom at his two restaurants in the south of France, Le Moulin de Mougins and L'Amandier de Mougins in Mougins, which have garnered five Michelin stars between them. In 1978, Roger published his first cookbook in French, *Ma Cuisine du soleil*, which reveled in the glories of Provençal cuisine. The success of this book led to another in 1986, *Entertaining in the French Style*. This lavish work also moved briskly off bookstore shelves. L'École de Moulin in Mougins is Roger's esteemed cooking school. He has trained many outstanding chefs there, and along with his staff, he also conducts classes for novice cooks. Roger frequently travels around the world as a guest chef, and his appearances at culinary events and premier restaurants always cause a stir.

on judy's kitchen: Roger enchanted my viewers. He grew more and more animated, his silvery hair gleaming and his ruddy complexion aglow, as he shared his recipes and techniques. The teamwork between Roger and Michel added a delightful French dimension to *Judy's Kitchen*. The huge volume of mail I received after this show confirmed my belief that viewers enjoyed these two superstar chefs as much as I did.

Roger prepared his famous Artichokes Barigoule Style and Baked Trout with Bay Leaves and Citrus Sauce. Michel dazzled everyone with his decadent chocolate sorbet and pistachio cookies—strictly kosher, of course.

menu

~ Artichokes Barigoule Style

~ Baked Fish with Bay Leaves and Citrus Sauce

~ Michel's Chocolate Sorbet

~ Pistachio Lace Cookies

Recently when Roger Vergé visited Los Angeles, he appeared as a guest chef for a week at Citrus Restaurant. He included this Provençal-style artichoke dish on the menu. It was a big hit, and I have been making it ever since. You can use either small or large artichokes, but the small ones are more appealing visually.

10 to 12 very small artichokes (or 4 large artichokes, quartered)

1   lemon, cut in half

Juice of 1 lemon

3   tablespoons olive oil

1   large onion, thinly sliced

2   carrots, thinly sliced

2   sprigs fresh thyme or ½ teaspoon dried thyme

1   bay leaf

6   garlic cloves, finely chopped

Kosher salt and freshly ground white pepper, to taste

1   cup dry white wine

1   small sprig basil, 5 leaves only

1   tablespoon chopped parsley

Trim the stems of the artichokes, leaving about 2 inches. Using a heavy chopping knife, cut about 1 inch off the tops. Tear away several layers of outside leaves close to the base, and trim the bottoms smoothly and evenly with a small sharp knife. As you work, generously rub each artichoke with the lemon half to prevent the flesh from darkening, and place in a bowl of cold water and lemon juice.

Heat the oil in a pot large enough to hold artichokes side by side. Sauté the onion and

carrots for 10 minutes, or until soft but not brown. Add the thyme, bay leaf, and half of the garlic.

Arrange the artichokes on top of the vegetables and sprinkle with salt and pepper. Pour in the wine and enough water to barely cover the artichokes. Cover and simmer for 20 minutes, adding more water as needed. Uncover, raise the heat to high, and reduce the broth to a syrupy liquid, about 15 minutes, or until artichokes are tender when pierced with a fork. (Turn artichokes periodically during this time.)

Place the basil, parsley, and the remaining garlic in a food processor or blender and chop fine. Just before serving, sprinkle the artichokes with salt and pepper again and carefully stir in the garlic mixture.

To serve, spoon the artichokes into shallow soup bowls with the vegetables and juices.

Serves 6   Pareve

Note: If necessary, this dish may be reheated. Do not add the garlic mixture until just before serving.

This delicate citrus sauce has perfect balance: The sharpness of the lemon and grapefruit is tempered by the oranges and olive oil. You can also serve this sauce with grilled fish.

2   whole red snappers (2 pounds each), head and tail intact

Kosher salt and freshly ground white pepper, to taste

5   bay leaves, fresh if possible

5   tablespoons olive oil

2   navel oranges

1   lemon

1   grapefruit

Season the fish inside and out with salt and
pepper. Cut 3 of the bay leaves into 8 small
triangles each. Using the point of a sharp knife,
make 12 tiny slits in the skin only on each side
of the fish and insert the bay leaf triangles.

Preheat the oven to 475°F.

Place a bay leaf in the cavity of each fish
and brush each all over with 1 tablespoon
olive oil. Marinate for 1 hour. Place the fish
on a wire rack and set it over a shallow
roasting pan half-filled with water. Bake for
20 minutes. Carefully turn the fish and
bake 15 minutes longer, or until fish flakes
easily when cut with a fork. (Cooking time
will vary slightly depending on the size of
the fish.)

While the fish is cooking, prepare the orange,
lemon, and grapefruit. Using a sharp knife, peel
each fruit close to the flesh, leaving no trace of
pith. Cut through each segment, detaching the
sections of fruit from the membrane. Do this
over a bowl, catching all the juices.

Combine the remaining 3 tablespoons olive
oil, the orange, lemon, and grapefruit segments
and their juices in a saucepan. Add salt and
pepper to taste. Warm over medium-high heat.
Be careful not to let the fruit get too hot, or it
will disintegrate.

To serve, carefully transfer the fish to a hot
platter. Serve the citrus sauce separately on
the side.

Serves 4   Pareve

michel's chocolate sorbet

Though made without any milk, cream, or eggs,
this super-smooth sorbet tastes as rich and
creamy as ice cream. The port really enhances the
sorbet's intense chocolate flavor.

3   cups unsweetened cocoa powder

2   cups sugar

1½ ounces semisweet chocolate, melted

1   cup port wine

Combine the cocoa and sugar in a large heavy
saucepan. Add 4 cups of water, a little at a
time, in a thin stream, mixing with a wire
whisk until well blended and smooth. Bring
to a boil and boil for 5 to 10 minutes, or until
thick. Stir in the melted chocolate and port.
Bring to a boil and simmer for about 4 minutes, or until thick, stirring constantly. Pour
into an 8-cup pitcher or bowl and place in a
larger bowl filled with ice and cold water. Mix
until cool. Remove bowl from ice. Cover with
plastic wrap and refrigerate.

Process in an ice cream machine according to
the manufacturer's instructions. Transfer the
sorbet to a covered container and freeze for at
least 1 hour for flavors to mellow. If frozen
solid, soften in the refrigerator and beat until
smooth and creamy before serving.

Makes about 2 quarts   Pareve

These delicate cookies have a rich nutty taste, with a subtle hint of orange.

1¼ cups pistachio nuts, toasted (see page 165)

¾ cup plus 2 tablespoons sugar

6 tablespoons unbleached all-purpose flour

6 tablespoons (¾ stick) unsalted butter, melted and cooled

¼ cup fresh orange juice

2 tablespoons Grand Marnier or other orange liqueur

Grind the pistachio nuts and sugar in a food processor, pulsing off and on until the nuts are coarsely chopped.

Blend the flour and the pistachio-sugar mixture in the bowl of an electric mixer. Add the butter, orange juice, and Grand Marnier and mix until evenly moistened. The dough will be wet and sticky. Lay a sheet of plastic wrap on a flat surface and roll out the dough into a 1-inch-wide log. Using the plastic wrap as an aid, roll up the dough in the plastic. Refrigerate until firm, about 6 hours.

Preheat the oven to 325°F.

Line several baking sheets with aluminum foil. Slice the dough into ⅛-inch-thick rounds. Placing the cookies 2 inches apart, arrange as many as will fit on the baking sheets.

Bake until well browned, about 12 minutes, rotating the baking sheets after 6 minutes. Cool, and carefully peel the cookies off the foil. Gently transfer to racks, in a single layer, to cool.

Makes about 8 dozen   Pareve

THOMAS A. KELLER
picasso of the plate

about the chef: In Napa Valley, Thomas Keller is one French laundryman who isn't French and doesn't do laundry. What he does do is cook and serve his food at the French Laundry, his Yountville restaurant.

In the middle of the wine country, Chef Keller is renowned for his extravagant four- to nine-course meals. They're filled with surprises, sometimes for the palate, other times for the eye. "It's important to make food look as good as it tastes," he says. He calls his dishes "pictures on plates." "My cooking is about using ingredients available in my backyard, in a way that expresses my personality and gives people pleasure," continues Thomas. He has long delighted patrons, as the chef of Rakel in Manhattan and as the executive chef of Checkers Hotel in downtown Los Angeles. Now that he's cooking in Napa Valley, I miss the opportunity to sample his food as often as I'd like. But at least I know that when I venture north, I'm sure to enjoy a great meal.

Thomas has a great sense of humor. Take, for example, his spin on shrimp cocktail. He fills a martini glass with chopped shrimp, then pours on tomato broth from a cocktail shaker. Not kosher? No problem. Thomas has substituted sea bass for the shrimp.

on judy's kitchen: Unlike some chefs, Thomas Keller is soft-spoken and modest. When I asked him to appear on my show, he told me how flattered he was to be asked. I was so pleased when he offered to prepare his Savory Cornets with Tuna Tartare. I first tasted this dish at a charity gala and knew how wonderful it is. We agreed that the sea bass cocktail and Poached Quail Egg on a Spoon were also good choices. They have become his signature appetizers, first at Checkers and now at the French Laundry.

The program was a big success, with a record number of viewers requesting recipes. While he cooked, Thomas shared many of his recipes, and we talked about how they could be adapted to a kosher kitchen. He felt that changing the ingredients to conform to the dietary laws would not interfere with the basic concept of the dishes. In fact, he said that is what his food is all about—the ability to substitute, which in this case means conforming to dietary restrictions.

menu

~ Keller's Festive Seafood Cocktail

~ Poached Quail Egg on a Spoon

~ Savory Cornets with Tuna Tartare

~ Warm Smoked Salmon with Potato Gnocchi

keller's festive seafood cocktail

This is Thomas Keller's signature appetizer, a wry martini. Minced and julienned vegetables replace the green olive, and tomato water replaces the martini mix. The presentation is dramatic, as are all of his dishes. Thomas served this starter on a round silver tray, with the intense-flavored tomato water in a cocktail shaker. He suggests drinking it like a martini.

The tomato water may be flavored in many ways, such as with chilies, or infused with herbs. Take care not to overcook the sea bass—the tomato water helps cook it.

6   tomatoes, finely diced

½   teaspoon salt

2   tablespoons olive oil

½   pound sea bass fillet, cut into thin slices

1   small carrot, minced

1   stalk celery, minced

½   red bell pepper, seeded and julienned

2   tablespoons minced chives

Puree the tomatoes in a food processor or blender. Add the salt. Spoon the tomato puree into a cheesecloth bag and let it hang over a bowl to extract the tomato water. Set aside.

Heat the olive oil in a nonstick skillet over medium heat and sauté the sea bass.

To serve, pour the tomato water into a cocktail shaker and place on a large tray with martini glasses. Spoon some of each vegetable into each glass, top with the sea bass, and sprinkle with chives. Pour the tomato water from the cocktail shaker into each glass at the table.

Serves 4   Pareve

poached quail egg on a spoon

The presentation of this hors d'oeuvre is remarkable. An oversized white plate holds a single, extra-large soup spoon filled with a poached quail egg and caviar. Thomas describes this dish as one bite of ecstasy bursting in your mouth.

6   quail eggs

1   teaspoon vinegar

4   tablespoons (½ stick) unsalted butter, melted

6   scant teaspoons salmon or whitefish roe

1   tablespoon minced chives, for garnish

Using a serrated knife, cut into the shell at the large end of the quail egg. Carefully open the shell and drop the egg into a small bowl. Repeat with the remaining eggs, each in its own bowl. Bring water and vinegar to a boil in a medium saucepan over high heat. Gently lower each egg into the boiling water and poach for 30 seconds, or until firm.

To serve, arrange 6 large soup spoons on 6 large plates. Using a slotted spoon, carefully transfer each poached egg to a soup spoon. Drizzle melted butter over the egg and top with roe. Sprinkle with chives.

Serves 6   Dairy

savory cornets with tuna tartare

I'll always remember the first time I met Thomas Keller because of one of his outstanding appetizer creations. It was at an American Institute of Wine and Food charity event. Tiny savory cones filled with Tuna Tartare were presented on a 24-inch-round disk, each in its own slot.

In the tartare, Thomas uses just enough shallots to heighten the delicate flavor of the tuna but not enough to overpower it. The roasted garlic puree used in the cornets can also flavor sauces or be spread on toast. It is known as *fettunta* in Italy.

6   tablespoons unbleached all-purpose flour

½   teaspoon salt

4   teaspoons sugar

2   egg whites

8   tablespoons (1 stick) unsalted butter, softened

1   teaspoon Fettunta (recipe follows)

Tuna Tartare (recipe follows)

10   tiny sprigs chervil, for garnish

Preheat the oven to 350°F.

Blend the flour, salt, sugar, egg whites, butter, and Fettunta in a food processor until the mixture comes together. Using a rubber spatula, transfer it to a small bowl.

To make a template, take a piece of thin cardboard and cut out a circle 4 inches in diameter. Lay the template flat on a nonstick or foil-lined baking sheet. Place a heaping tablespoon of dough in the center of the circle and spread it thin using a metal spatula. Keep the spatula flat, almost parallel to the table. (An offset spatula is handy for this task.) The dough should be evenly spread, about ⅟₁₆ inch thick. If the dough is not spread uniformly, the thinner part will burn during baking. Remove the cardboard and use it to make another disk next to the first one. (For easier handling, make 2 cornets at a time.) Bake for about 6 minutes, or until pliable. Immediately wrap each disk around a metal cornet cone. Return to the oven and bake until brown, about 4 minutes. Slide off the mold and set aside. Just

before serving, fill with Tuna Tartare. Garnish with a tiny sprig of chervil.

Makes about 10   Dairy

Note: If you don't have metal cornet cones, double the recipe and bake the disks for 4 minutes, or until golden brown. Leave them flat and sandwich the tuna between 2 rounds.

Makes about 5 filled sandwiches

fettunta (roasted garlic paste)

1   head garlic, cloves separated but not peeled

Preheat the oven to 250°F.

Wrap the garlic cloves in foil and pinch the foil to seal. Bake for 1 hour, or until soft. Squeeze each garlic clove to release the pulp into a glass bowl. Cover with plastic wrap and refrigerate. (The garlic paste will keep for 1 week in the refrigerator.)

Makes about ¼ cup   Pareve

tuna tartare

½   pound tuna, julienned

2   shallots, minced

Pinch of wasabi powder or fresh horseradish (see Note)

2   tablespoons olive oil

Salt and freshly ground black pepper, to taste

1   teaspoon fresh lemon juice (optional)

Combine the tuna, shallots, wasabi powder, olive oil, salt, and pepper in a bowl. Stir in the lemon juice.

Makes about 1 cup   Pareve

Note: Wasabi is available in the Japanese section of most supermarkets.

warm smoked salmon with potato gnocchi

This innovative combination of salmon, Italian gnocchi, and port syrup can be served as a first course or as a main course for lunch or dinner. Potatoes and smoked salmon are a perfect marriage. I still remember a stew of boiled smoked salmon collars and potatoes we used to have for Sunday lunch years ago.

The port syrup is just as delicious with fruit or ice cream as with savory foods like poultry or meat.

Gnocchi (recipe follows)

1   cup port wine

1   tablespoon olive oil

6   pieces (4 ounces each) smoked salmon, skins reserved

2   to 3 cups whole milk

¼   cup chopped chives, for garnish

12   chive tips, 3 inches long, for garnish

Prepare the gnocchi and keep warm.

Heat the port in a heavy saucepan over medium heat and cook until reduced to a syrup, about 10 minutes. Do not boil. Let cool.

In a nonstick skillet, heat the oil and cook the salmon skin until crispy. Set aside.

Place the salmon in a baking dish large enough to hold it comfortably. Heat the milk, but do not allow it to boil. Pour enough milk over the salmon to cover and let it steep for 3 minutes.

To serve, spoon the gnocchi onto serving plates. Drain the salmon and arrange on top of the gnocchi. Garnish with crisp salmon skin, chopped chives, and chive tips. Drizzle 2 teaspoons of the port syrup around the gnocchi.

Note: Balsamic vinegar may be substituted for the port syrup. See page 166 for a kosher balsamic-style vinegar.

Serves 6   Dairy

gnocchi (italian potato dumplings)

2   pounds russet potatoes, scrubbed

1½   cups all-purpose flour

3   egg yolks

Salt and freshly ground black pepper, to taste

1½   tablespoons olive oil

1   tablespoon unsalted butter

2   tablespoons grated Parmesan

Boil the potatoes in a large pot over medium heat until soft. Peel and pass through a potato ricer into a large mixing bowl. While still warm, add the flour, egg yolks, salt, and pepper. Mix well. Spoon the potato mixture into a pastry bag fitted with a #8 plain tip and pipe the mixture into long ropes on a floured surface. Cut into ¾-inch pieces and roll the gnocchi, one by one, over the tines of a fork to produce a ribbed effect. Blanch the gnocchi in boiling salted water until they rise to the surface. Plunge into ice water. Drain and pat dry.

(Gnocchi may be frozen at this point.)

To reheat, pour a small amount of water into the bottom of a sauté pan. Add the gnocchi, olive oil, and butter. Cook for 1 minute. Sprinkle with the Parmesan.

Makes about 7 dozen gnocchi   Dairy

chef's secrets

❧ To open a quail egg, use a sharp serrated knife and make a cut into the shell at the large end of the egg. Carefully open the shell and allow the egg to drop into a bowl. Do not crack the egg on the edge of a glass or bowl or the yolk may break.

❧ Adding salt to sliced or pureed tomatoes helps extract flavorful water from the tomatoes. The tomato water can be used in salad dressing and soups.

❧ Warm milk poured over smoked salmon helps extract the salt.

EVAN KLEIMAN
italian-meets-jewish cuisine

about the chef: Most chefs have had to adjust their cooking style to fit the kosher format of my show. Not Evan Kleiman. Her specialty is Italian cuisine and history, with a special emphasis on Italian-Jewish culture. In fact, she prepares an Italian Passover seder menu at Angeli Café, her Los Angeles bistro, every year.

Evan took an atypical route to success. While many chefs spend years training in culinary academies and apprenticing under famous chefs, Evan created a name for herself in a different fashion—and it happened without even trying. Evan began to cook at a very young age, preparing meals for herself and her working mother. Each night when her mom returned home, a hot homemade dinner was waiting for her on the table. Later, Evan developed entrepreneurial traits. In high school, she started selling her homemade cookies, and she worked her way through college as a caterer. But she yearned to pursue a film career, and she went forward with that goal in mind. Eventually, though, she realized her heart was in cooking. She halted her studies to work at Mangia restaurant in Los Angeles as night chef and kitchen manager. Logging more than one hundred hours in her first week, Evan was hooked. She had found her niche.

Soon word of her talent spread, and she was hired by Verdi Ristorante di Musica in Santa Monica to become the executive chef. Evan felt the city had a need for a modern Italian family restaurant serving light, simple food that was stylish and affordable. In December 1984, she opened the casual-chic Angeli Café, which is still going strong. Indeed, many credit Evan for creating a restaurant concept that's been widely copied. She now spends most of her time as a culinary instructor, food consultant, and cookbook author.

on judy's kitchen: Evan was a star guest. She was well organized and quickly established herself as an expert in the art of kosher cooking. We had a wonderful time comparing Jewish holiday menus.

Evan brought several kinds of kosher fish to the studio, and offered descriptions and cooking tips for each. Evan has a gift for teaching, and she has strong opinions about food—from olive oil to black versus white pepper. The audience was clearly intrigued with this culinary expert, both for her knowledge and her clarity.

menu

~ Panzanella (Bread Salad)

~ Radicchio-Orange Salad

~ Pesce in Carpione (Marinated Whitefish with Pine Nuts)

panzanella (bread salad)

Panzanella is a classic salad of Florence. It should be made with day-old coarse-textured country-style Italian or French bread. The salad is made with lots of tomatoes, red onions, and cucumbers.

2   tomatoes, peeled, seeded, and cut into ½-inch dice

1   to 2 tablespoons capers, drained

½   cup olive oil, or more to taste

¼   cup red wine vinegar, or more to taste

Kosher salt and freshly ground black pepper, to taste

½   loaf day-old country-style Italian or French bread, cut into ½-inch slices and crusts removed

3   cucumbers, peeled, halved lengthwise, seeded, and cut into ½-inch dice

½   small red onion, thinly sliced

1   red or yellow bell pepper, seeded and cut lengthwise into very thin strips

In a large bowl, mix together the tomatoes, capers, oil, vinegar, salt, and pepper. Arrange a layer of bread slices in a wide, shallow bowl or on a large platter. Scatter the cucumbers, onion, and bell pepper strips over the bread. Pour a ladleful of the tomato mixture over the bread and vegetables. Top with a layer of bread slices. Continue layering until all the ingredients are used, ending with the vegetables and tomato mixture.

Cover with plastic wrap and refrigerate for at least 2 hours before serving to allow the bread to absorb the liquid from the vegetables and tomato mixture. Sprinkle with more oil and vinegar if needed.

Serves 4 to 6   Pareve

radicchio-orange salad

Serve this refreshing salad before or after the main course.

3   heads radicchio

2   oranges

Olive oil

Balsamic vinegar

Salt and freshly ground black pepper, to taste

Carefully separate the radicchio leaves from the heads and wash the leaves. If they are too bitter, soak in a large bowl of water to cover for 20 minutes. Drain and dry well. Refrigerate.

Using a sharp knife, peel the oranges, taking care to remove all the pith. Use a paring knife to remove individual segments from the membranes. Remove any seeds. Arrange the radicchio leaves on individual salad plates, tearing very large leaves in half. Arrange the orange segments on top of the radicchio leaves. Drizzle olive oil and balsamic vinegar over each salad. Season with salt and pepper.

Serves 4 to 6   Pareve

pesce in carpione (marinated whitefish with pine nuts)

This dish comes from an ancient tradition of using acidic marinades to preserve fish. The longer the fish remains in the marinade, the more flavorful it becomes. The sweetness of the onion and raisins and the bolder flavors of the wine vinegar, mustard, and saffron make a dramatic contrast.

Evan suggests serving pickled fish in place of gefilte fish for the seder dinner.

⅓ cup golden raisins

¼ cup plus 2 tablespoons olive oil

1½ onions, thinly sliced

¾ cup white wine vinegar

1 tablespoon Dijon mustard

1 shallot, minced

2 garlic cloves, minced

Juice of ½ lemon

Salt and freshly ground black pepper, to taste

Vegetable oil, for frying

1 pound whitefish fillet, cut into 4 to 6
   equal portions

1 cup all-purpose flour

1 head butter lettuce or radicchio

¾ cup toasted pine nuts

Soak the raisins in warm water to cover for about 15 minutes. Drain and set aside.

Heat the 2 tablespoons olive oil in a nonstick skillet over medium heat and sauté the onions, stirring occasionally, for about 20 minutes, or until tender. Raise the heat, add the vinegar, and simmer for a few minutes to reduce the liquid slightly. Add the raisins and remove from the heat.

Combine the mustard, shallot, garlic, lemon juice, and the remaining ¼ cup olive oil in a glass bowl. Season with salt and pepper and set aside.

Heat about 1 inch vegetable oil in a nonstick skillet over medium heat until very hot but not smoking. Dust the fish lightly in the flour, season with salt and pepper, and fry until golden. Drain on paper towels. Place the fish in a shallow glass dish and top with the onion mixture. Pour the lemon mixture over the fish and onions and cover with plastic wrap. Marinate for at least 3 hours, preferably overnight. Bring back to room temperature before serving.

To serve, separate the lettuce into leaves, wash, and dry them. Arrange on individual plates. Lift the fish, topped with the onion mixture, out of the marinade and arrange on the lettuce leaves. Sprinkle with pine nuts.

Serves 4 to 6   Pareve

chef's secrets

❧ Professional chefs cook fish on very high heat for good results.

❧ The key to success when cooking fish at home is pairing the right type of fish with the best cooking technique.

❧ Lake Superior whitefish and John Dory are lean, flaky, and tender; suitable for broiling and quick sautés.

❧ Salmon and tuna have more fat and a firmer texture, which make them adaptable to a wide variety of cooking techniques, especially grilling, which is rough on delicate fish. Grilling fish with the skin on is best.

❧ Fish such as red snapper and rock cod (often sold as red snapper) are rich and flavorful, and perfect for soups, stews, and braising.

❧ Chilean sea bass is a foolproof fish—lots of moisture and wonderful texture—very hard to overcook.

JOHANNE KILLEEN AND GEORGE GERMON
inventive italian cuisine

about the chefs: Johanne Killeen and George Germon rank as one of America's premier culinary couples. These two chefs are compatible in and out of the kitchen. Together they own Al Forno in Providence, Rhode Island, an establishment that has become a destination for Northeast food lovers.

Johanne and George both trained as artists at the Rhode Island School of Design. Johanne studied photography; George focused on sculpting and pottery. But this twosome discovered their true passion lay with more toothsome matters. At their restaurant, Johanne specializes in desserts, while George oversees the savory fare. They've been working together successfully for nearly twenty years.

on judy's kitchen: The first time I met George and Johanne was on the set, just before taping the show. It was friendship at first sight. Their philosophy—a most contagious one—is to have fun with food and life.

I regret that they live in Providence and my husband and I are in Los Angeles. However, we've discovered a great place to meet—Italy. We often get together in our home away from home, and we're looking forward to visiting them in their soon-to-be-completed house in France.

The recipes the two prepared on the show are indicative of the cuisine at Al Forno restaurant and are showcased in their cookbook, *Cucina Simpatica*. Because George and Johanne are so organized and work so well together, they were able to make many dishes in a short amount of time. Johanne provided most of the direction; George did most of the cooking. They completed their dishes in a seamless fashion.

menu

~ Mushroom Salad with Parmesan Cheese

~ Crunchy Fennel Salad

~ Spaghettini with Watercress Aglio e Olio

~ Conchiglie with Mushrooms and Radicchio

~ Mascarpone Custard with Fruits of the Season

mushroom salad with parmesan cheese

All three salads were inspired by a meal George and Johanne had enjoyed in Bologna, Italy. All the ingredients are available in supermarkets.

¾   pound white button mushrooms

¼   teaspoon kosher salt

1   teaspoon fresh thyme leaves or 24 to 30 fresh Italian flat-leaf parsley leaves

1   piece (4 to 6 ounces) Parmigiano-Reggiano

2   lemons

6   to 8 tablespoons olive oil

Freshly cracked pepper, to taste

Wipe the mushrooms to remove any dirt clinging to them. Trim the stem ends, and cut the mushrooms vertically into paper-thin slices.

Distribute a layer of mushrooms on 4 to 6 individual salad plates and sprinkle with a pinch of salt and some thyme. With a stainless steel vegetable peeler, shave a layer of Parmigiano-Reggiano over the mushrooms. Repeat the process with the remaining mushrooms, salt, herbs, and cheese, adding new layers until all the ingredients are used.

Cut one of the lemons into 4 to 6 wedges for garnish. Squeeze the juice of the other lemon. Drizzle 1 to 1½ tablespoons of olive oil over each salad, pour on lemon juice, sprinkle with freshly cracked pepper, and garnish with lemon wedges.

Serves 4 to 6   Dairy

crunchy fennel salad

Fennel is an aromatic but underused vegetable, tasting a little like anise. Be sure to save the trimmings from the fennel bulb to use for stock.

4   large fennel bulbs

½   teaspoon kosher salt

1   piece (4 to 6 ounces) Parmigiano-Reggiano

½   cup Italian flat-leaf parsley leaves

2   lemons

6   to 8 tablespoons olive oil

Cut off the feathery leaves and stalks of the fennel. Trim the root ends and discard. With a sharp knife, cut the fennel lengthwise into paper-thin slices. Distribute half of the fennel among 4 to 6 salad plates, sprinkle with salt, and cover with a layer of Parmigiano-Reggiano, shaved directly over the salad with a vegetable peeler. Garnish with parsley leaves. Repeat the process, making additional layers, until all the ingredients are used.

Cut one of the lemons in 4 to 6 wedges and squeeze the juice of the other lemon. Drizzle the salads with olive oil and lemon juice and garnish with lemon wedges.

Serves 4 to 6   Dairy

spaghettini with watercress aglio e olio

When watercress is combined with spaghettini at the last moment, it retains its bright green color.

½   cup virgin olive oil

2   tablespoons minced garlic

1   teaspoon kosher salt

1   cup Vegetable Stock (page 166)

1   pound spaghettini, preferably imported

2   cups chopped watercress

Fill a large pot with 5 quarts of salted water and bring to a rolling boil.

Heat the olive oil in a large sauté pan over medium heat. Add the garlic and sauté for about 2 minutes, stirring occasionally, until it turns a rich, golden color. Immediately add the salt and stock. Bring to a boil and reduce by half. Keep the sauce warm over very low heat.

Drop the spaghettini into the boiling water and cook until it's still quite firm, 4 to 5 minutes. Drain in a colander. Transfer to the garlic mixture in the sauté pan. Add the watercress and toss for about 2 minutes, or until the spaghettini is al dente. Serve immediately.

Serves 6 to 8 as an appetizer or 4 as a main course   Pareve

conchiglie with mushrooms and radicchio

This is the Rolls Royce of pastas! Four cheeses combined with cream, pasta shells, and mushrooms make for a luxurious meatless meal. These individual casseroles can be assembled in advance and baked just before serving. I have served this dairy dish as the main course for our Shavuot dinner.

6   ounces shiitake mushrooms

8   tablespoons (1 stick) unsalted butter

1   teaspoon kosher salt

2   cups finely shredded radicchio

2½ cups heavy cream

½   cup freshly grated Parmigiano-Reggiano

½   cup coarsely shredded fontina

½   cup crumbled gorgonzola

2   teaspoons ricotta, whisked with a fork until smooth

6   sage leaves, chopped

1   pound conchiglie (pasta shells), preferably imported

Preheat the oven to 500°F.

Fill a large pot with 5 quarts of salted water and bring to a rolling boil.

Wipe the shiitakes clean. Remove the stems and reserve for another use. Slice the caps about ¼ inch thick. Melt 6 tablespoons of the butter in a large skillet over medium heat. Add the mushrooms and ¼ teaspoon salt. Sauté, stirring frequently, until the mushrooms are cooked through, 3 to 5 minutes. Combine the sautéed mushrooms, radicchio, cream, the 4 cheeses, and remaining salt in a large mixing bowl.

Boil the conchiglie for 4 minutes, drain, and add to ingredients in the bowl. Toss to combine.

To serve, divide the pasta mixture among 4 to 6 individual gratin dishes (1½- to 2-cup capacity). Dot with the remaining 2 tablespoons butter and bake until bubbly and brown on top, 7 to 10 minutes.

Serves 4 to 6   Dairy

mascarpone custard with fruits of the season

Johanne used fresh figs when she prepared this dish on television, as they were in season. Follow Johanne's rule and use whatever fresh fruits are available and at their peak of freshness.

1   cup milk

2   egg yolks

½   cup granulated sugar

¼   cup unbleached all-purpose flour

¾   cup heavy cream

1   teaspoon vanilla extract

½   cup mascarpone or ricotta cheese (see Note)

4½   cups fresh raspberries or other fresh
       seasonal fruit

3   teaspoons confectioners' sugar

Preheat the oven to 425°F.

Scald the milk in a heavy saucepan.

Beat the egg yolks in a medium bowl until light and pale in color. Add the sugar, 1 tablespoon at a time, beating well after each addition. Fold in the flour and beat until smooth.

Pour the scalded milk into the egg yolk mixture in a slow stream, beating constantly until smooth. Return the mixture to the saucepan and cook, stirring, until it comes to a boil. Boil for 2 minutes, remove from heat, and transfer to a mixing bowl. Cool to room temperature. Refrigerate, covered, for at least 1 hour, or until well chilled.

To finish the custard, whip the cream with the vanilla until it thickens and begins to hold its shape. Whisk the chilled yolk mixture until smooth. Fold the mascarpone into the yolk mixture and gently fold in the whipped cream. Refrigerate until ready to use. (The custard may be refrigerated for up to 2 days.)

To serve, arrange 6 individual gratin dishes (1 cup each) on a baking sheet. Spoon ¼ cup of custard into each dish and divide the raspberries among them. Sift 2 teaspoons of the confectioners' sugar over the berries and top with the remaining custard. Sift 1 teaspoon confectioners' sugar over the tops. Bake for 5 to 7 minutes, or until heated through and berries have released some of their juices.

Preheat the broiler.

Remove the custards from the oven and place under the broiler. Brown for 1 minute, watching carefully to make sure the tops don't burn. Serve immediately.

Serves 6   Dairy

Note: If using ricotta, blend until smooth in a food processor.

chef's secrets

♨ Mushrooms should never be washed, just wiped with a damp towel.

♨ If possible, always use pasta imported from Italy and imported Parmigiano-Reggiano cheese.

♨ Use kosher salt exclusively.

JOSIE LE BALCH

cooking runs in the family

about the chef: Josie Le Balch has had a close source of inspiration for her career—her father. Known throughout Los Angeles as Chef Gregoire, her dad owned a charming restaurant where he championed French cuisine for many years. Not only did he prepare excellent classic dishes, he was also a patient and personable cooking instructor. I know: He was one of my early French cooking teachers.

Josie began her career working for Wolfgang Puck at the original Ma Maison and for the legendary Jean Bertranoux at L'Ermitage. After tours in France and Italy, she returned to Southern California in 1980 to become executive chef of Remi in Santa Monica. This Italian eatery was soon named one of the best new restaurants in the city.

Now Josie is at the helm of Saddle Peak Lodge in Malibu canyon. The restaurant is nestled in the mountains between the San Fernando Valley and the ocean and resembles a cozy hunting lodge. Josie's adventurous cooking, in keeping with the ambience, features game. Saddle Peak Lodge has been widely acclaimed by local critics, and the establishment is consistently filled with contented diners.

on judy's kitchen: Josie's appearance on *Judy's Kitchen* represented her television debut. She was concerned she might have little to say that was interesting or important. Not a chance! A lively conversation flowed naturally, contrary to her fears.

Josie peppered her segment with many cooking tips for the home cook; for example, she demonstrated the art of tossing a sauce in a skillet. This is no easy task the first time out, and Josie recommended that viewers practice this technique with clean pebbles from the garden. She also demonstrated how one sauce can be put to use in different recipes. For her Goat Cheese and Tomato Appetizer, the sauce was chunky. Then she pureed it for filled Italian crepes, Crespelle with Ricotta and Spinach. For penne, she transformed the basic sauce by adding olives, capers, and crushed red pepper, which gave it a flavor boost.

Josie's cooking style is clearly her own: it's based on her extensive background in classic French and Venetian-Italian cuisine. "Cooking knows no boundaries," she confided to the viewers. "As long as you understand which flavors and textures work well together, experimentation can be endless."

menu

~ Goat Cheese and Tomato Appetizer

~ Crespelle with Ricotta and Spinach

~ Penne with Piccante Sauce

goat cheese and tomato appetizer

Chef Gregoire, Josie's father, who was one of the pioneer French chefs in Los Angeles, always greeted guests at his restaurant with a slice of quiche. This goat cheese appetizer is Josie's way of welcoming her patrons.

The tomato sauce is chunky and spicy. Double the recipe and you can also use it for the penne and crespelle recipes.

Basic Tomato Sauce (recipe follows)

Herbed Goat Cheese (recipe follows)

Minced parsley, for garnish

Olive oil, for drizzling

Prepare the Basic Tomato Sauce and the Herbed Goat Cheese.

Preheat the broiler.

To serve, cover the bottom of 12 small (3-inch), shallow custard cups or ramekins with tomato sauce. Use an ice cream scoop to place cheese mixture in the center of each cup and heat under the broiler for about 5 minutes, or until the top is brown. Do not let the cheese mixture melt. Sprinkle with parsley and drizzle with a little olive oil.

Serves 12   Dairy

basic tomato sauce

2   tablespoons olive oil

4   garlic cloves, chopped

2   small white onions, finely diced

1   can (28 ounces) whole plum tomatoes, with liquid

4   cups fresh tomatoes, peeled, seeded, and chopped

8   whole basil leaves, sliced

Salt and freshly ground black pepper, to taste

Heat the oil in a large skillet over medium-high heat. Add the garlic and sauté until golden, 1 to 2 minutes. Add the onion and sauté until soft and translucent, about 5 minutes. Add the canned and fresh tomatoes and basil and simmer until soft, about 5 minutes. Using a wire whisk or fork, mash the tomatoes. Simmer over low heat until the mixture thickens into a sauce, about 45 minutes. Season with salt and pepper. Let cool. (The sauce may be covered with plastic wrap and stored in the refrigerator for 2 to 3 days and in the freezer for up to 1 month.)

Makes about 4 cups   Pareve

herbed goat cheese

Other flavorful cheeses such as blue cheese or Stilton cheese can be substituted for goat cheese.

8   ounces montrachet or other goat cheese

8   ounces cream cheese, room temperature

¼   cup mascarpone (optional)

1   garlic clove, minced

1   tablespoon chopped basil

Salt, to taste

2   tablespoons olive oil, or more to taste

Combine the montrachet, cream cheese, mascarpone (if using), garlic, basil, salt, and olive oil in the large bowl of an electric mixer. Mix

until smooth, about 2 minutes. Add more olive oil if needed for smoother consistency. Cover with plastic wrap and refrigerate about 1 hour.

Makes about 3 cups   Dairy

crespelle with ricotta and spinach

Crespella are Italian crepes. I always marvel at how versatile crepes are. And how easy to make. This recipe is most appealing, with the filled crespelle presented on a pool of tomato sauce and garnished with creamy cheese rosettes. Think of blintzes with an Italian accent.

5   eggs

2   egg yolks

1   cup milk

½   cup heavy cream

1¾   cups whole wheat or unbleached all-purpose flour

Pinch of salt

1   tablespoon olive oil

4   tablespoons (½ stick) unsalted butter, melted

Ricotta-Spinach Filling (recipe follows)

Pureed Tomato Sauce (recipe follows)

Herbed Goat Cheese, for garnish (page 46)

Beat the eggs and egg yolks in the bowl of an electric mixer. Blend in the milk and cream. Add the flour, salt, and oil and blend well. Pour into a fine-mesh strainer set over a large bowl and allow the batter to slowly drip through. Or push the batter through the strainer with a rubber spatula. The batter should be the consistency of heavy cream. If it's too thick, add a little more milk. It can be used immediately or covered with plastic wrap, refrigerated, and used the next day.

Brush a well-seasoned crepe pan with butter and heat. When the pan is hot, pour in about 3 tablespoons of batter and tilt and rotate the pan to distribute it evenly and thinly, pouring off any excess. The first crepe will be thicker than the rest. Cook until the underside is lightly browned around the edges, 2 to 3 minutes. Turn and cook on the other side 1 to 2 minutes longer. Repeat with the remaining batter, stacking the cooked crepes on a dish with a piece of wax paper between each one.

Preheat the oven to 325°F. Line a baking sheet with foil.

Spread about 2 tablespoons of the Ricotta-Spinach Filling over the entire surface of each crepe. Fold ½ inch of each side over the filling and roll up tight. Cut each roll into 4 pieces and place on the baking sheet. Bake until heated through, about 5 minutes.

To serve, heat the tomato sauce and spoon some in the center of each plate. Arrange 4 or 5 rolled crepes, cut side up, on top of the sauce. Fill a pastry bag fitted with a rosette tip with the cheese mixture and pipe a rosette on each crepe.

Serves 12   Dairy

ricotta-spinach filling

1   pound ricotta

8   ounces spinach, steamed, squeezed dry, and finely chopped

Freshly grated nutmeg

Salt, to taste

Place the ricotta in a strainer set over a medium bowl for 30 minutes to drain.

Mix the drained ricotta cheese, spinach, nutmeg, and salt in a large bowl. Cover with plastic wrap and refrigerate.

Makes about 3 cups   Dairy

pureed tomato sauce

2   cups Basic Tomato Sauce (page 46)

1   carrot, coarsely chopped

2   stalks celery, coarsely chopped

1   small onion, coarsely chopped

Place the tomato sauce in a large saucepan and add the carrot, celery, and onion. Simmer, covered, until the vegetables are soft, about 1 hour. Puree in a food processor until smooth.

Makes about 2 cups   Pareve

penne with piccante sauce

Josie prepared the tomato sauce for the goat cheese appetizer and took it one step farther to make a hot tomato sauce for pasta. This penne is a simple but satisfying main course that needs only a crisp green salad and red wine to accompany it.

2   cups (8 ounces) penne rigate

1   tablespoon olive oil

1   garlic clove, chopped

1   cup Basic Tomato Sauce (page 46)

5   kalamata olives, pitted and halved

8   capers, drained

Crushed red pepper, to taste

4   sprigs rosemary, for garnish

1½   tablespoons unsalted butter

¾   cup grated Parmesan cheese, or to taste

Fill a large pot with salted water and bring to a rolling boil. Add the penne and boil just until al dente, about 10 minutes, since the penne will continue to cook when simmered in sauce. Drain and spread on a baking sheet.

Heat the oil in a nonstick skillet over medium-high heat. Add the garlic and sauté until golden, 1 to 2 minutes. Add the tomato sauce, olives, and capers, and cook for 1 minute. Add the penne, red pepper, and rosemary. Cook until heated through, about 3 minutes. Do not overcook. Blend in the butter and 2 tablespoons of the Parmesan.

To serve, spoon the penne onto individual plates and garnish with rosemary. Pass a bowl of the remaining grated Parmesan cheese on the side.

Serves 4   Dairy

chef's secrets

To add subtle garlic flavor to a sauce, crush each clove and sauté it whole in olive oil. Remove it or leave it in while the sauce is simmering, then discard. This method gives the sauce a nice garlic flavor that is not bitter or overpowering.

When using only fresh tomatoes in a recipe instead of a combination of canned and fresh, the sauce tends to be more acidic. Add brown sugar to taste to counterbalance the acidity.

To boil any dried pasta in advance, undercook it and spread it on a baking sheet. The pasta will continue to cook when simmered in sauce.

about the chefs: What Italian flavor we had on this show! Two young chefs from Bergamo, Italy, who now work for Piero Selvaggio in Southern California, prepared traditional Italian dishes from two of Piero's famous restaurants. Angelo Auriana has been the chef at Valentino Ristorante in Santa Monica for more than ten years, and Luciano Pelligrini is the chef at Posto in the San Fernando Valley. Piero brought both chefs over from Italy and helped them launch their careers. He is so proud of them that he calls them his children.

Piero Selvaggio, originally from Sicily, is known in Los Angeles as the Unofficial Italian Ambassador. With the help of his wife, Stacy, Piero owns and manages Valentino Ristorante, Primi un Ristorante, and Posto. He is also the consultant for the Theme restaurant at the Los Angeles Music Center.

Under Piero's watchful eye, Angelo Auriana creates innovative menus faithful to Italian culinary tradition. After an apprenticeship in San Pellegrino, a famous spa north of Milan, Angelo trained at several restaurants in Bergamo, where he developed his own style. In stints around Italy, he also learned the cuisine of the country's other regions before coming to the United States in 1984. A Florida vacation led to two years in the kitchen of an old-style Italian restaurant; a subsequent vacation brought him to Los Angeles, where he met Piero. "It was like a marriage," he says. Angelo helped open Primi restaurant in West Los Angeles. He possesses a light touch and an adventurous palate.

Raised in the Lombardy region of northern Italy, Luciano Pelligrini graduated from the prestigious San Pellegrino hotel school and cooked in some of Italy's finest restaurants, among them Vecchia Lugana in Lake Garda and Locanda Dell'Angelo in Bergamo, before coming stateside to head the kitchen of Piero Selvaggio's restaurant Primi. Prior to opening Posto, where he is the chef, Luciano spent six months in Italy studying the art of focolare (open-air grilling) and sausage making.

on judy's kitchen: Although both chefs were a little shy about talking on camera with their heavy Italian accents, they did very well. I don't think they realized their own charm. They performed as a team, each preparing a dish and then stepping back to allow the other to make his—not without a little kidding around. Since cooking on *Judy's Kitchen*, these two charming chefs no longer worry about their accents and eagerly accept teaching assignments.

menu

~ Angelo's Warm Sea Bass Salad

~ Baked Sea Bass with Polenta Triangles

~ Luciano's Two-in-One Risotto

angelo's warm sea bass salad

Angelo slices the sea bass as thin as if he were slicing smoked salmon and then quickly sautés it. Wash and chill the salad greens before sautéing the sea bass so they will be ready when the fish is done.

6   tablespoons olive oil

1½ pounds sea bass fillet, skinned, boned, and thinly sliced

1   cup dry white wine

1   garlic clove, thinly sliced

¼   pound kalamata olives

½   cup thinly sliced celery

½   cup thinly sliced red bell pepper

1   tomato, diced

5   basil leaves, minced

Salt and freshly ground black pepper, to taste

3   cups mesclun, or mixed baby greens such as arugula and red leaf

Olive oil, for garnish

Heat 3 tablespoons of the olive oil in a non-stick skillet over medium heat until crackling. Quickly sauté the fish slices on both sides until golden, about 1 minute. Do not overcook. Remove the fish from the pan, discard the oil, and put the fish back in the pan. Add the remaining olive oil, wine, garlic, olives, celery, bell pepper, tomato, and basil. Add salt and pepper. Simmer until the wine is reduced to half.

To serve, arrange the mixed greens in the center of 6 plates and place the sea bass on top. Spoon the warm sauce and vegetables over the greens and fish and drizzle a little olive oil over each salad.

Serves 6   Pareve

baked sea bass with polenta triangles

Dried cod is traditionally used in this northern Italian recipe from Bergamo, Angelo's hometown, though he substituted fresh sea bass in this rendition. You could also use Lake Superior whitefish. For Angelo, preparing polenta was a task close to his heart, since they always serve it in Bergamo.

Polenta is not new. Made from white or yellow cornmeal, it was a staple in Italy long before pasta and risotto became popular in the United States. It is most versatile and may be served soft (the consistency of hot cereal) or firm; the firm polenta may be grilled, baked, or fried. Polenta makes a great appetizer or first course. As a main course, serve generous portions of soft polenta topped with sautéed or grilled vegetables.

It seems every family—Italian or Jewish—has a polenta-type dish. When I was growing up, cornmeal mush, served with spoonfuls of sour cream on top, was our version.

Polenta Triangles (recipe follows)

2   tablespoons olive oil

3   large white onions, cut in half and thinly sliced

6   sea bass fillets (about 8 ounces each), skins on

Salt and freshly ground black pepper, to taste

Paprika, to taste

1   cup Fish Stock (page 167)

1   cup dry white wine

1   cup half-and-half or milk

½   cup chopped parsley, for garnish

Prepare the polenta triangles and keep warm.

Preheat the oven to 450°F.

Heat the olive oil in a saucepan over medium heat and sauté the onions, stirring frequently, for 4 minutes or until soft. Transfer the onions to a large ovenproof pan or baking dish. Season the sea bass fillets with salt, pepper, and paprika and arrange them, skin side up, on top of onions. Pour the stock, wine, and half-and-half over the fish, making sure the liquid covers the fish. Bake for about 10 minutes, or until the fish flakes easily with a fork.

To serve, arrange the polenta triangles in the center of 6 plates, spoon the onions in the center of the triangles, and arrange the fish on top. Sprinkle with parsley.

Serves 6   Pareve

polenta triangles

2   teaspoons salt

2   cups cornmeal

¼   cup olive oil, for frying (optional)

Fill a large heavy pot with 2 quarts water, add the salt, and bring to a boil over high heat. As soon as the water comes to a gentle simmer, start pouring in the cornmeal in a steady stream, stirring constantly with a wooden spoon to avoid lumps. Cook for 3 minutes, lower the heat, and continue to cook on low heat, stirring often, for about 20 minutes, or until thick.

Pour the polenta into a buttered baking dish and spread evenly. Cool until firm. Cut into 12 to 16 triangles. In a skillet, heat the olive oil over medium heat and brown the polenta triangles on both sides.

Serves 6 to 8   Dairy

luciano's two-in-one risotto

Risotto can be made with nothing more than parmesan stirred in or with vegetables, meat, fish, or poultry as well. For the show, Luciano prepared risotto two ways: one with sautéed mushrooms, the other with sautéed vegetables. He used fresh porcini mushrooms from Oregon. "The test of a good risotto is to shake it," Piero says. "If it moves like small waves in the sea, it's perfect. If the risotto is too stiff, add more broth."

Reconstituted dried porcini or shiitake mushrooms are good replacements for fresh wild mushrooms. Parmesan cheese stirred into the rice at the last minute gives it a rich, creamy taste.

Sautéed Mushrooms (recipe follows)

Sautéed Vegetables (recipe follows)

3   tablespoons olive oil

¼   small onion, minced

2   cups arborio rice

½   cup dry white wine

5 to 6 cups warm Pareve Chicken Stock (page 167) or Vegetable Stock (page 166)

2   tablespoons unsalted butter

½   cup grated Parmesan

Prepare the mushrooms and the vegetables and keep warm.

In a large heavy sauté pan, heat the olive oil over medium heat. Add the onion and sauté for 1 to 2 minutes, or until it begins to soften. Add the rice and stir with a wooden spoon for 2 to 3 minutes, or until all the grains are well coated with oil. (Pick up a couple of grains with your fingertips; if they're too hot to handle, the rice is toasted.) Add the wine and stir into the rice until completely absorbed.

Add ½ cup of the warm stock at a time, stirring constantly until each addition is almost completely absorbed before adding the next ½ cup. Continue adding stock until the rice is cooked through but still al dente, about 15 minutes. Remove from heat and quickly stir in the butter and ¼ cup of the parmesan. Transfer half of the risotto to another pot. Add 2 cups of the mushrooms to one batch and 2 cups of the vegetables to the other and mix well.

To serve, spoon a portion of each risotto into heated shallow soup bowls and garnish with the reserved mushrooms and vegetables. Sprinkle with the remaining parmesan cheese and serve at once.

Serves 6 to 8   Dairy

sautéed mushrooms

2   tablespoons olive oil

1   garlic clove, chopped

3   cups sliced fresh mushrooms or dried mushrooms (see Note)

Salt and freshly ground black pepper, to taste

Heat the olive oil in a skillet over medium heat and sauté the garlic and mushrooms, stirring frequently, until soft. Season with salt and pepper. Remove from heat and keep warm.

Makes about 2 cups   Pareve

Note: To use dried porcini or shiitake mushrooms, soak 1 cup (1 ounce) dried mushrooms in warm water for 20 minutes. Remove the mushrooms from the soaking liquid, chop coarsely, and add to the risotto. Carefully pour the soaking liquid into the risotto, so the sediment remains in the bottom of the bowl,

or filter it through cheesecloth. Continue cooking the risotto until the soaking liquid is absorbed, then start adding the stock.

sautéed vegetables

2   tablespoons olive oil

¼   cup diced onion

1   garlic clove, chopped

3   cups sliced vegetables, such as green beans, asparagus, red bell peppers, celery, zucchini, and carrots, or a combination

2   tablespoons chopped basil

Salt and freshly ground black pepper, to taste

Heat the olive oil in a large skillet over medium heat and sauté the onion and garlic for 1 minute. Add the vegetables, reduce heat to low, and sauté, stirring constantly, until tender but firm, about 5 minutes. Sprinkle with basil and season with salt and pepper. Remove from heat and keep warm.

Makes about 2 cups   Pareve

chef's secrets

❧ To make risotto in advance, follow the recipe, adding the liquid and mixing for eight minutes. Then spoon the risotto into a glass baking dish, spread it evenly to 1 inch thick, and set aside. Fifteen minutes before serving, return the risotto to pan and continue cooking as directed in the recipe.

❧ To make *arancine* (rice balls) with leftover risotto, roll it into 2-inch balls, flatten and fry on both sides in hot oil until a crust forms. Serve hot. You can serve these as latkes for Hanukkah.

CELESTINO DRAGO
sicilian sensation

about the chef: Celestino Drago always dreamed of opening his own restaurant, even as a child in Sicily. A self-taught cook, Celestino grew up on a farm just outside Palermo in a family of cooks. By the age of nineteen, he had become the executive chef of Pierino Ristorante, near Pisa in Tuscany. But when he was offered an airline ticket to Southern California—and a job with Los Angeles restaurateur Orlando Orsini—Celestino packed his bags in a hurry. He became the chef at Chianti Cucina, a charming Italian restaurant, where he was greeted with much acclaim. In 1985, Celestino fulfilled his dream by opening his own restaurant, Celestino in Beverly Hills. He was among the first chefs to introduce L.A. food lovers to Sicilian fare. Today, Celestino is one of Los Angeles's most highly regarded chefs—and one of the most popular. His Drago Ristorante in Santa Monica is packed nightly. And his two Il Pastaio restaurants, in Beverly Hills and Pasadena, have developed a loyal following of devotees who appreciate the casual pasta-risotto –based cuisine and the comfortably chic neighborhood setting. At the Beverly Hills restaurant, Celestino's brother Giacomino Drago heads the kitchen. He recently received an award naming him the "best young entrepreneur in Beverly Hills."

Celestino's family is of upmost importance to him. Not only is Giacomino involved in the restaurant operations, but so are two other brothers, Tanino and Calogero. At all of Celestino's establishments, it's truly a family affair. Now with his own new family, can we expect wife Leslie and baby Olivia soon to show up in the restaurants?

on judy's kitchen: Who can resist the charm of Celestino Drago? His smile is so warm, and he always displays an irresistible, mischievous nature. Celestino is a chef who loves to have fun in the kitchen. Before we taped the show, Celestino and I were already good friends. We often cooked together at home. So the cameras became invisible. We just worked and laughed together as if no one was watching. This relaxed atmosphere made for a magical show.

Celestino prepared his signature heart-shape ravioli filled with ricotta and swiss chard. He also made a potato-crusted whitefish. What a fabulous dish! Thinly sliced potatoes are placed over the fillets to resemble fish scales. This entree is surprisingly easy to make and serves as a dramatic main course for entertaining.

menu

~ Ravioli Hearts with Sage and Butter Sauce

~ Whitefish with Potatoes

~ Pasticcini alle Nocciole (Hazelnut Cookies)

ravioli hearts with sage and butter sauce

Celestino is famous for his heart-shape ravioli. When he prepares them at special events, the crowds go wild. Make your own pasta using Celestino's recipe and your crowd will go wild too. Swiss chard adds a distinctive color and flavor to the ricotta filling.

Fresh Pasta Dough (recipe follows)

1   egg mixed with 1 tablespoon milk, for egg wash

Ricotta and Swiss Chard Filling (recipe follows)

Sage and Butter Sauce (recipe follows)

¼   cup grated parmesan

Sage leaves, for garnish

Select 2 equal size pasta sheets. Paint 1 sheet with eggwash. Spoon the Ricotta and Swiss Chard Filling into a pastry bag and pipe out mounds about 1 teaspoon each, 1 inch apart over the first sheet of pasta. Lay the second sheet over the first, pressing between the mounds of filling. Using a heart-shape cookie cutter, cut into heart-shape ravioli.

Fill a large pot with salted water and bring to a gentle boil. Cook the ravioli for 3 to 4 minutes, or until tender. Drain very carefully. Gently place the ravioli in the Sage and Butter Sauce and mix to coat.

To serve, spoon into heated plates and sprinkle with parmesan. Garnish with sage leaves.

Serves 8 to 10   Dairy

fresh pasta dough

4   cups all-purpose flour

1   teaspoon salt

4   eggs

2   teaspoons olive oil

Place the flour and salt on a wooden pastry board or in a large bowl and make a well in the center. Break the eggs into the well and add the olive oil. With a fork, beat the eggs and oil, gradually drawing the flour from the edge of the well and incorporating it into the egg mixture to form a dough that can be gathered into a ball. Transfer to a floured board if in a bowl.

Knead the dough for 5 to 10 minutes, working in extra flour as necessary, until it is no longer sticky. Wrap the dough in plastic wrap and let rest in the refrigerator for about 2 hours.

Remove the dough from the refrigerator and roll it out with a pasta machine (see Note) or rolling pin to the desired thickness. Dough can be cut into fettuccine, tagliolini, or lasagna widths, or used as flat sheets to make ravioli.

Serves 8   Pareve

Note: Set the rollers at the widest opening. Divide the dough into 4 parts for easier handling. Working with 1 part at a time, flatten the dough with the palm of your hand into a thick strip no wider than the machine. Dust it lightly with flour and crank it through the machine. Fold it in half or thirds, press it down with your fingertips, dust with flour, turn it 90 degrees (a quarter-turn) and run it through the machine again. Repeat this process 3 or 4 more times, dusting with flour, until the dough is smooth, elastic, and no longer sticky. Now the dough is ready to stretch into a long sheet.

Set the machine to the next opening, bringing the rollers closer together, and run the dough through. This time, do not fold or turn the dough. Set the rollers another notch closer and run the dough through again. Continue rolling the dough, through a smaller opening each time, stopping just before the next-to-narrowest setting. (The dough strip will become very long, so allow ample work space, or cut the dough into shorter sheets as you go along.)

For stuffed pasta, follow the directions for the ravioli hearts on page 56, using the pasta sheets while they are still moist. Keep the sheets covered until ready to use. For noodles, let the pasta dry for about 15 minutes before cutting, depending on the temperature and humidity of the kitchen.

ricotta and swiss chard filling

1½ cups ricotta cheese

4   egg yolks

½   cup grated Parmesan

½   cup cooked, drained, and chopped swiss chard

Combine the ricotta, eggs, and Parmesan in a large bowl. Mix in the chard. Set aside.

Makes about 3 cups   Dairy

sage and butter sauce

3   tablespoons unsalted butter

20 sage leaves

1   cup heavy cream

Salt, to taste

Heat 1 tablespoon of the butter in a saucepan over medium heat. Add the sage leaves and sauté until golden, about 2 minutes. Add the cream and salt. Simmer until sauce is reduced to three quarters of its original volume, about 5 minutes. Remove from heat, add the remaining 2 tablespoons butter, and whisk until the butter dissolves. Keep warm.

Makes about 1½ cups   Dairy

whitefish with potatoes

Thinly sliced potatoes become the "scales" of the fish. The sautéed shiitake mushrooms add a rich but subtle flavor.

Sautéed Shiitake Mushrooms (recipe follows)

1   tablespoon unsalted butter or margarine

1   tablespoon olive oil

4   medium peeled potatoes, very thinly sliced

1   tablespoon minced thyme

4   whitefish fillets (5 ounces each)

¼   cup peeled, seeded, and diced tomatoes, for garnish

Olive oil, for drizzling

12 basil leaves, for garnish

Prepare the mushrooms and keep warm.

Heat ¼ tablespoon of the butter and ¼ tablespoon of the oil in a nonstick skillet over medium heat. Place a quarter of the potatoes, overlapping the slices, in a single layer, in the center of the skillet, approximating the size of a fish fillet. Sprinkle with thyme, then place the fish on top. Sauté on very low heat until the potatoes are golden brown and crisp. Remove from heat. Using a spatula or 2 spoons, carefully turn the fish over. Brown for 1 minute or longer, depending on the thickness of the fillet. Repeat this process with the remaining fish and potatoes.

To serve, place the sautéed mushrooms in the middle of 4 warm plates, top with the fish and potatoes, and sprinkle the diced tomatoes around the fish. Drizzle with olive oil and garnish with basil leaves. Serve hot.

Serves 4   Dairy

sautéed shiitake mushrooms

1   tablespoon olive oil

1   tablespoon unsalted butter

1   teaspoon minced thyme

1   pound fresh shiitake mushrooms, cleaned

Salt and freshly ground black pepper, to taste

2   tablespoons balsamic vinegar

Remove the stems of the mushrooms and cut the caps into slices. Set aside.

Heat the olive oil and butter in a skillet over medium-high heat. Add the thyme, mushrooms, salt, and pepper and sauté for 3 to 4 minutes, until soft. Add the balsalmic vinegar and cook until it evaporates. Make sure the oil is very hot before you add the mushrooms. Season with salt and pepper. Remove from the heat and keep warm.

Makes 1 pound   Pareve

pasticcini alle nocciole (hazelnut cookies)

In Italy, these cookies are known by the name of *buoni ma bruti*, or good but ugly. The joke does not detract from the ultra-crisp goodness of these cookies. This is one of the cookies I bake during Hanukkah. Packed in fancy tins, they make great gifts.

4   egg whites

1   cup confectioners' sugar

1   cup hazelnuts, toasted, peeled, and coarsely ground (see page 165)

Oil, for baking sheets

Preheat the oven to 350°F. Line several baking sheets with foil and brush with oil.

Place the egg whites in a clean, dry bowl and whip until firm but not dry. Add the sugar, beating in a little at a time until incorporated. Mix in the hazelnuts. Transfer the mixture to a medium saucepan over low heat and mix with a wooden spoon until the egg white mixture pulls away from the bottom and sides of the pan, about 3 minutes. Remove the pan from heat and let the egg white mixture rest for 10 minutes.

Place ½-tablespoon mounds of the hazelnut mixture on a baking sheet, leaving about 1 inch between each mound. Bake for 20 minutes, or until golden brown. Using a metal spatula, carefully transfer cookies to a rack. Cool.

Makes 4 dozen cookies   Pareve

BRADLEY OGDEN

real american cooking

about the chef: Talk about American cooking and you've got to mention Bradley Ogden, one of the masters of modern American cuisine. An honors graduate of the Culinary Institute of America in Hyde Park, New York, Bradley first came into the spotlight at the American Restaurant in Kansas City, Missouri. Everyone wanted to know who was cooking such elegant food based on simple but intense flavors.

Bradley became chef of Campton Place, a sophisticated boutique hotel in San Francisco. For six years, he captured media attention for his straightforward American cooking with a contemporary twist. He then moved on to become co-owner and executive chef of Lark Creek Inn, a rustic restaurant in Larkspur, California. The success of Lark Creek Inn was almost instantaneous and has spawned the opening of casual Lark Creek Café. Bradley is also a chef-owner in One Market Restaurant, an innovative San Francisco dining establishment.

Bradley claims his appreciation of quality American cuisine developed during his childhood in Michigan, where he was exposed to so many wonderful ingredients like garden-fresh tomatoes and corn, cherries, apples, and freshwater fish. By taking these ingredients, and other local specialties, and giving them a spin like few other chefs, Bradley has helped to change the face of American cooking.

on judy's kitchen: With his boyish charm and charismatic grin, Bradley quickly endeared himself to my audience, preparing dishes from his *Bradley Ogden's Breakfast, Lunch, and Dinner* cookbook, which we transformed into kosher fare. He won over my camera crew too by treating them to his famous hot chocolate cream, which his mother often made for him when he was growing up. After sipping the comforting drink, the crew became his biggest fans.

It's impossible for anyone to resist Bradley's Buttery Scones, Spiced Pear Butter, and Salmon Hash. These dishes are the same he serves at home for Sunday brunch with his wife, Jody, and their three sons. I think his prune fritters would make a most special addition for a holiday brunch during the eight days of Hanukkah.

~ Prune Fritters with Lemon and Orange Curd

~ Buttery Scones

~ Spiced Pear Butter

~ Salmon Hash

buttery scones

Scones are almost as popular here as they are in England. Sometimes currants are added, but Ogden stands by his classic, melt-in-your-mouth version. One bite, and you'll know why.

4   cups cake flour

2   tablespoons baking powder

2   tablespoons sugar

1½ teaspoons salt

2   teaspoons grated orange zest

8   tablespoons (1 stick) cold unsalted butter, cut into pieces

1½ cups heavy cream

½   cup buttermilk

Preheat the oven to 400°F.

Sift together the flour, baking powder, sugar, and salt in a large bowl. Stir in the orange zest. Add the cold butter to the flour mixture and, using a fork or pastry blender, cut the mixture until it resembles coarse meal. In another bowl, mix together the cream and buttermilk and add all at once to the dry ingredients.

Stir the dough with a rubber spatula just until it is moistened. Turn out onto a floured board and pat out to a ¾-inch-thick rectangle. Using a 3-inch biscuit cutter, cut into rounds. Place the rounds 1 inch apart on a baking sheet. Bake for 20 minutes, or until puffed and lightly browned.

Makes about 1 dozen   Dairy

spiced pear butter

Simplicity itself! Aromatic with spices and subtly flavored with pears, this spread is much more elegant than apple butter.

2   pounds firm ripe pears, such as Comice, unpeeled

¾   cup apple cider

¼   cup firmly packed light brown sugar

⅛   teaspoon ground cinnamon

⅛   teaspoon ground allspice

Pinch of ground cloves

Pinch of ground nutmeg

2   tablespoons fresh lemon juice

Core the pears and cut into large chunks. Combine the pears, cider, brown sugar, spices, and lemon juice in a 4-quart heavy-bottomed saucepan. Bring to a boil over high heat, reduce heat to low, and simmer, stirring occasionally, for about 1 hour. The mixture should be thick and most of the liquid evaporated.

Remove from heat and puree in a food mill or food processor. Cover with plastic wrap and refrigerate.

Makes about 1¼ cups   Pareve

salmon hash

Try this fresh salmon dish for a festive Sunday brunch, along with some of Bradley's other specialties, in place of the predictable smoked salmon with cream cheese. But don't forgo the bagels!

¾ pound fresh salmon fillet

Kosher salt and freshly ground black pepper, to taste

2   tablespoons fresh lemon juice

2   cups cold water

2   to 3 medium russet potatoes

6   tablespoons clarified butter (see page 165)

¾   cup thinly sliced yellow bell pepper

¾   cup thinly sliced red bell pepper

¾   cup sliced yellow Spanish onion

¾   cup sliced leeks, white part only (1 x ⅛ inch)

½   teaspoon chopped thyme

½   teaspoon minced savory

½   teaspoon minced tarragon

1   tablespoon chopped Italian flat-leaf parsley

Kosher salt and freshly ground pepper, to taste

2   tablespoons unsalted butter

Lemon wedges, for garnish

Remove the skin from the salmon fillet and cut the fish into 12 pieces. Season with salt and pepper and refrigerate.

Combine the lemon juice and cold water in a large bowl. Peel and shred the potatoes and place in water. Just before frying, drain and squeeze out excess liquid from potatoes. In a large nonstick skillet, heat the clarified butter and spread the potatoes loosely and evenly on the bottom of the pan. Brown the potatoes and drain on paper towels. Set aside and keep warm.

Pour out all but 1 tablespoon butter from the pan. Add the yellow and red bell peppers, onion, and leeks and sauté for 3 to 4 minutes, or until the vegetables are softened. Stir in the herbs, salt, and pepper to taste. Stir in the potatoes. Keep warm.

Melt the unsalted butter in a skillet over high heat and sauté the salmon until golden brown, about 2 minutes. Do not allow the pieces of salmon to touch or they will steam and not sear. Turn the salmon over and add the potato mixture to the skillet. Continue to cook until the salmon is just medium-rare, 1 to 2 minutes.

To serve, place the vegetables on 6 warm plates and top with the salmon.

Serves 6   Dairy

JOACHIM SPLICHAL
potatoes with pizzazz

about the chef: Think potatoes. Potato lasagne, potato ravioli, unfried french fries, potato truffle chips—who would think that a German chef could rocket to American stardom because of his potato creations? Well, Joachim Splichal could, and did. His spins on spuds were amazing. And his other concoctions weren't too shabby either.

One of the most acclaimed chefs in America today, Joachim began his career early, working with his parents in their hotel/restaurant in Germany. After attending the Hotel and Management School in Montreux, Switzerland, he trained with some of Europe's brightest stars. He studied with Louis Outhier at the esteemed L'Oasis in Napoule-Plage, France. At the age of twenty-three, he was hired as sous chef by Jacques Maximin for Chantecler Restaurant in Nice's Hôtel Negresco. He received numerous awards, including first prize for Youngest and Most Creative Chef from the Cercle Epicurean Society in Germany.

Joachim came to the United States in 1981 to cook for the newly established Regency Club in Los Angeles. He then moved to downtown Los Angeles to head Seventh Street Bistro. By the time he opened Beverly Hills's Max Au Triangle in 1984, the whispers about Joachim's talent turned to roars. In 1989, he opened Patina Restaurant in Hollywood with Christine, his French wife. Honors abounded, including an award from the James Beard Foundation for Best Chef in California. Joachim's restaurants now include Pinot Bistro, Pinot Hollywood, Pinot at the Chronicle, and Patinette at the Museum of Contemporary Art. His newest enterprise is Pinot Blanc in Napa Valley. Christine and Joachim also run the Patina catering division, which many consider the city's finest. *Patina Cookbook: Spuds, Truffles and Wild Gnocchi*, written by Joachim, is a runaway success.

on judy's kitchen: This may have been Joachim's first appearance on television. He was extremely serious, but a great sport. While preparing his signature Potato Lasagne with Wild Mushrooms, his face lit up as he discussed his interest in potatoes. He said that potatoes were as exciting to him as pasta was to Italians. He also made his corn blinis with marinated salmon, the signature appetizer at Patina. I often serve the blinis at home along with potato latkes for our family Hanukkah celebration.

menu

~ Corn Blini Sandwich with Gravlax

~ Red Bell Pepper Soup with CLT Sandwiches

~ Potato Lasagne with Wild Mushrooms

corn blini sandwich with gravlax

This dish has been on the menu since the day the doors opened at Patina. Delicate corn blini are layered with marinated salmon and served on a pool of sour cream sauce. Boiling the corn with the shallots and cream adds a delicate flavor to the blini. Joachim sometimes substitutes wild rice for the corn in the blini batter.

Remember that the marinated salmon has to be prepared one to two days in advance.

Sour Cream–Chive Sauce

1   cup sour cream

1   red bell pepper, roasted, seeded, and diced (see page 165)

1   tablespoon minced chives

3   cups fresh or frozen corn kernels (5 to 6 ears of corn)

3   tablespoons unsalted butter

1½ tablespoons minced shallots

1   cup heavy cream

⅔   cup whole milk

2   eggs

1   cup unbleached all-purpose flour

1½ teaspoons baking powder

½   teaspoon salt

2   tablespoons minced chives

Unsalted butter, melted, for frying

Gravlax (recipe follows)

¼   cup chopped chives, for garnish

To make the Sour Cream–Chive Sauce, blend the sour cream, bell pepper, and chives together in a small bowl. Cover with plastic wrap and refrigerate.

Blanch the corn in boiling water. Drain and set aside.

Heat 2 tablespoons of the butter in a skillet over medium heat and sauté the shallots until soft, about 3 minutes. Add the corn and cream and cook over low heat for 15 to 20 minutes. Puree in a food processor.

Beat the milk and eggs together in a small bowl. In a large mixing bowl, using a wire whisk, mix together the flour, baking powder, and salt. Whisk in the milk mixture and remaining 1 tablespoon butter. Mix in the corn puree and chives.

Brush a nonstick skillet with butter and heat. Pour in 1 heaping tablespoon of the batter for each blini and cook until golden brown, about 1 minute. Using a spatula, carefully turn the blini and cook until golden brown. Brush the skillet with more butter for each batch.

To serve, spread a large spoonful of Sour Cream–Chive Sauce in the center of each plate, spreading evenly with the back of the spoon. Arrange 1 blini in the center of the sauce, top with paper-thin slices of marinated salmon, and cover with another blini. Garnish by sprinkling chives around the sandwich.

Makes 20 sandwiches   Dairy

gravlax (marinated salmon)

2   pounds whole salmon, skin on, scaled and boned to make 2 fillets

12 sprigs fresh dill

¼   cup kosher salt

¼ cup sugar

2 tablespoons fennel seeds

2 tablespoons cracked white peppercorns

Place one of the salmon fillets, skin side down, in a shallow glass baking dish or casserole. Place the dill on top of the fillet. Set aside.

Combine the salt, sugar, fennel seeds, and peppercorns in a small bowl. Sprinkle over the dill. Top with the other salmon fillet, skin side up. Cover with plastic wrap and then with a platter slightly larger than the salmon but smaller than the baking dish. Top the platter with cans of food or bricks to weight it down. Marinate in the refrigerator for 24 hours, or until the moisture is leached from the salmon.

To serve, remove the salmon from its marinade, scrape away the dill and seasonings, and pat dry with paper towels. Place skin side down on a carving board and slice paper thin at an almost horizontal angle, detaching each slice from the skin.

Serves 10   Pareve

red bell pepper soup with "clt" sandwiches

Joachim makes a German-style celery broth for the soup base, but a vegetable broth works well too. Clever little cheese, lettuce, and tomato sandwiches—CLTs—are served on the side. When Joachim serves this soup at Patina he often puts roasted red pepper pieces and herbs in the bottom of the soup bowl and then ladles the soup over.

4 tablespoons (½ stick) unsalted butter

1 small onion, coarsely chopped

1 medium leek, white part only, coarsely chopped

1 stalk celery, coarsely chopped

5 red bell peppers, roasted, peeled, seeded, and diced (see page 165)

1 large russet potato, peeled and sliced ¼ inch thick

¼ cup dry white wine

6 cups Celery Broth (recipe follows) or Vegetable Stock (page 166)

1 cup heavy cream

1 sprig basil, finely chopped

Salt and freshly ground white pepper, to taste

CLT Sandwiches (recipe follows)

Heat the butter in a large saucepan over medium-high heat and sauté the onion, leek, celery, red peppers, and potato until soft. Add the wine and cook until the wine reduces, about 2 minutes. Add the broth and cook, uncovered, for 10 to 15 minutes. Puree the mixture in a food processor or blender. Add the cream and basil and mix well. Transfer to saucepan. Season with salt and pepper. Reheat before serving.

Serve with CLT Sandwiches.

Serves 10   Dairy

1   tablespoon unsalted butter

10 stalks celery, coarsely chopped

1   large onion, coarsely chopped

2   leeks, white part only, coarsely chopped

6   garlic cloves, unpeeled

2   sprigs thyme

2   sprigs parsley

4   cups dry white wine

Salt and freshly ground white pepper, to taste

Melt the butter in a large saucepan over low heat and add the celery, onion, leek, garlic, thyme, and parsley. Sauté over medium-low heat, stirring occasionally, for about 30 minutes, or until vegetables are soft. Do not let the vegetables brown. Add the wine, increase the heat slightly, and simmer for 1 hour. Add 4 cups water, salt, and pepper and simmer for 20 minutes more. Strain stock through a sieve, pressing hard on solids to extract all their flavor. Discard the vegetables and set the stock aside. (The broth may be refrigerated for up to 3 days or frozen in ½-cup containers for future sauces.

Makes about 6 cups   Dairy

clt sandwiches

½   pound frozen puff pastry, thawed in the refrigerator overnight

1   egg yolk, beaten

2   tablespoons sesame seeds

Sour cream

10 leaves lettuce, preferably baby lettuce, torn

2   tomatoes, thinly sliced

1   cup shredded monterey jack cheese

Preheat the oven to 350°F.

Roll out a sheet of puff pastry on a work surface. Using a scalloped cookie cutter, cut ten 1-inch circles. Brush with egg yolk and sprinkle with sesame seeds. Bake for 10 minutes, or until puffed and golden. Slice each round in half and brush the bottom half with sour cream. Top with a lettuce leaf, a slice of tomato, and cheese. Cover with the top half of the round. Serve with soup.

Makes 10 sandwiches   Dairy

potato lasagne with wild mushrooms

Joachim is noted for his unusual potato recipes. Here he surprises us with a towering creation—seven layers of potatoes and mushrooms, topped with a delicate chive sauce.

8   tablespoons (1 stick) unsalted butter, melted

Salt and freshly ground black pepper, to taste

2   large russet potatoes

4   cups assorted mushrooms, such as shiitake, oyster, button, or chanterelle mushrooms, sliced and stems removed

1   large shallot, minced

¼   cup minced parsley

¼   cup minced chives

Chive Sauce (recipe follows)

Preheat the oven to 350°F.

Line 2 baking sheets with parchment or wax paper and lightly brush with melted butter. Sprinkle with a little salt and pepper.

Peel and trim the potatoes into 3 x 2-inch blocks. Slice each block crosswise into ⅛-inch-thick rectangles. Each potato should yield 9 to 10 slices. Arrange the slices in a single layer on baking sheets. Brush with butter and sprinkle with salt and pepper. Cover the potatoes with another sheet of parchment or wax paper and bake for 5 minutes, or until soft. Set aside.

Heat the remaining melted butter in a skillet over medium-high heat. Add the mushrooms and sauté until all liquid has evaporated, about 5 minutes. Add the shallot, parsley, and chives, and mix well. Season with salt and pepper and remove from heat.

On another baking sheet, make 4 individual lasagnes by layering first a sheet of potato, then a thick layer of mushroom mixture, then another sheet of potato. Make 4 potato layers and 3 layers of mushroom mixture, ending with a potato layer on top. Place another baking sheet on top of the lasagnes. Weight it down. Let the lasagnes compress for 1 hour, otherwise they will fall apart.

To serve, reheat the lasagnes until warm in a low (300°F) oven for about 5 minutes. Using a metal spatula, transfer the lasagnes to individual heated plates. Spoon the sauce over and around each serving.

Serves 4   Dairy

chive sauce

1¼ cups Celery Broth (page 67)

12 tablespoons (1½ sticks) unsalted butter, at room temperature, cut into pieces

Salt and freshly ground black pepper, to taste

1 tablespoon minced chives

1 medium tomato, peeled, seeded, and diced (see page 166)

Bring the broth to a boil in a saucepan over medium-high heat. Add one third of the butter, stirring until melted. Pour the mixture into a food processor or blender. Blend at high speed. Add the remaining butter and blend thoroughly. Season with salt and pepper. Transfer to a bowl and stir in the chives and diced tomato.

Makes about 2 cups   Dairy

STEPHAN PYLES

a texan at home in the white house

about the chef: Born in western Texas, Stephan began his culinary journey at the age of eight, working in his parents' truck stop cafés. While flipping burgers, never did he dream he would one day cook at the White House.

But Stephan didn't become seriously interested in cooking as a career, until he fell in love with French food on a post-graduate trip to France. Inspired by such renowned chefs as Roger Vergé and Alain Chapel, he decided to make cooking his career. He worked in small restaurants and studied every cookbook he could find. Then he got lucky: He was asked to assist the visiting chefs at Robert Mondavi's Great Chefs of France Cooking School in Napa Valley. As he worked with living legends like Georges Blanc and Michel Guérard, his passion for cooking intensified.

In 1983, Stephan and his partner, John Dayton, opened Routh Street Café, which featured contemporary Southwest cuisine, in Dallas. Stephan's talent was quickly noticed. In its first year, the restaurant received numerous awards and praise from local and national magazines. He was the first Texan named to *Cook's* magazine's Who's Who of Cooking in America. *Bon Appétit* magazine credits Stephan with almost single-handedly changing the Texas cooking scene. Today he is chef of Star Canyon restaurant in Dallas, and the praise continues to pour in. "My food is a little cowboy and a little Southern," says Stephan, "with Creole, Latin, Mexican, and Southwestern influences."

on judy's kitchen: Stephan was more than a little reluctant to be a guest on my show. He didn't feel comfortable because he knew nothing about kosher cooking. I told him that since he had already mastered so many cuisines, what was one more? When, at the end of the show, I asked Stephan how he liked cooking kosher, he admitted that he loved the challenge of adapting his recipes to suit the dietary laws.

menu

~ Pumpkin–White Bean Chowder with Garlic Croutons and Pomegranate Crème Fraîche

~ Goat Cheese–Almond Chile Rellenos with Dried Apricots

pumpkin–white bean chowder with garlic croutons and pomegranate crème fraîche

This recipe takes a little time, but you can prepare it in steps. The beans can be soaked, drained, and boiled in advance, and the pumpkin may also be prepared the day before. Stephan says sweet potatoes may be substituted for the pumpkin; and the juice of an orange, reduced to two table-spoons, for the pomegranate glaze to flavor the crème fraîche.

2½ quarts Pareve Chicken Stock (page 167) or Vegetable Stock (page 166)

1½ cups dried white beans, soaked overnight and drained

1 pumpkin or banana squash (about 5 pounds)

1 tablespoon corn oil

1 onion, diced

2 stalks celery, diced

1 carrot, diced

1 red bell pepper, seeded and diced

1 yellow bell pepper, seeded and diced

2 garlic cloves, minced

2 tablespoons chopped thyme

¼ cup white wine

Pomegranate Crème Fraîche (recipe follows), for garnish

Garlic Croutons (recipe follows), for garnish

¼ cup chopped chives, for garnish

Preheat the oven to 350°F. Line a baking sheet with foil.

Bring 2 cups of the stock to a boil in a large pot over high heat. Add the beans, lower the heat, and simmer, covered, for 30 to 45 minutes, or until tender. Set aside.

Cut the pumpkin into 4 pieces and remove the seeds. Bake three of the pieces, skin side down, on the baking sheet for 30 minutes. Peel the reserved piece, cut into ¼-inch dice, and boil until tender, about 1 minute. Drain and plunge into cold water. Drain and set aside.

Heat the oil in a large saucepan over medium heat and sauté the onion, celery, carrot, red and yellow peppers, garlic, and thyme for 3 to 5 minutes, or until the vegetables turn translucent. Add the wine and remove the pan from heat. Add the baked pumpkin to the vegetables. Add the remaining 2 quarts stock, bring to a boil, reduce heat and simmer, partly covered, for 45 minutes, or until cooked through.

While the soup is simmering, prepare the Pomegranate Crème Fraîche and Garlic Croutons.

Puree the soup in a blender, strain, return to a saucepan and add the reserved diced pumpkin and white beans. Season with salt and heat through.

To serve, ladle into soup bowls, garnish with the crème fraîche, pomegranate seeds, crou-tons, and chives.

Serves 6 to 8   Dairy

pomegranate crème fraîche

1 large pomegranate

½ cup crème fraîche or sour cream

1 tablespoon heavy cream

Cut the pomegranate into quarters and remove the seeds from 1 quarter for garnish. Squeeze the other 3 quarters into a saucepan. You should have about 1 cup of juice. Bring to a boil and simmer until reduced to a syrupy glaze, 2 to 3 minutes. Transfer to a bowl and whisk in the crème fraîche and heavy cream.

Makes about ¼ cup   Dairy

garlic croutons

3   tablespoons olive oil

1   tablespoon roasted garlic (see page 165)

Salt, to taste

4   slices French or sourdough bread, crust removed and cut into ½-inch cubes

Preheat the oven to 350°F.

Combine the olive oil, roasted garlic, and salt in a mixing bowl. Add the bread cubes and mix thoroughly. Spread on a baking sheet and bake for 5 to 7 minutes, or until golden brown.

Makes about 1 cup   Pareve

goat cheese–almond chiles rellenos with dried apricots

Stuffed chilies are very much a part of Southwest cuisine. Deep-frying a chili before peeling it keeps it from becoming too soft and helps retain its bright green color.

Almond Sauce (recipe follows)

Pico de Gallo (recipe follows)

Vegetable oil, for deep-frying

8   anaheim chilies

Ice water

2   garlic cloves, roasted and mashed (see page 165)

6   ounces goat cheese, crumbled, or brie or cream cheese

¾   cup grated Monterey Jack cheese

1   tablespoon chopped shallots

1   tablespoon chopped cilantro

1   tablespoon chopped basil

1   tablespoon chopped marjoram

½   cup diced dried apricots

2   tablespoons almonds, toasted and chopped (see page 165)

Salt and freshly ground black pepper, to taste

1   egg

2   tablespoons heavy cream

1   cup yellow cornmeal, for dredging

8   sprigs cilantro, for garnish

Prepare the Almond Sauce and Pico de Gallo and set aside.

Fill a large pot with oil and heat to 325°F. Drop a chili into the hot oil and fry until the skin puffs up. Drop into a bowl of ice water and peel. Repeat with the remaining chilies. Carefully slit each chili down one side and remove the seeds, leaving the stem attached.

Combine the garlic with the goat cheese, jack cheese, shallots, cilantro, basil, marjoram, apricots, and almonds in a large bowl. Season with salt and pepper, and mix well. Stuff the chilies with the mixture, taking care not to overfill. Close the chilies, arrange on paper towels on a dish, and refrigerate for at least 30 minutes.

Beat the egg and cream in a shallow bowl. Put the cornmeal on a plate or piece of wax paper. Dip the stuffed chilies in the egg mixture and coat with cornmeal. (The chilies can be refrigerated at this point.)

Heat 3 t o 4 inches of oil in a skillet and fry the stuffed chilies until golden brown.

To serve, spoon Almond Sauce on each plate and arrange a stuffed chili on top. Spoon the Pico de Gallo on the side. Garnish with sprigs of cilantro.

Serves 8   Dairy

almond sauce

1	cup heavy cream
½	cup toasted sliced almonds (see page 165)
1	tablespoon roasted garlic (page 165)
2	tablespoons Pareve Chicken Stock (page 167)

Salt, to taste

Heat the cream in a large saucepan over medium heat and reduce to ¾ cup, whisking frequently. Transfer to a blender, add the almonds, roasted garlic, and stock and blend until smooth. Season with salt and strain through a fine-mesh strainer. Keep warm or reheat when ready to serve.

Makes about 1¾ cups   Dairy

pico de gallo (rooster's beak tomato salsa)

5	ripe tomatoes
1	tablespoon chopped cilantro
1	garlic clove
½	cup minced onion

Juice of ½ lime

2	small serrano chilies, seeded and minced

Salt, to taste

With a sharp paring knife, remove the outer wall of flesh from each tomato, leaving the skin intact. Discard the pulp and seeds or use for soups, stews, or stocks. Cut the tomato flesh into ¼-inch dice and place in a medium bowl. Add the cilantro, garlic, onion, lime juice, serrano chilies, and salt. Let stand for 30 minutes before serving.

Makes about 3 cups   Pareve

chef's secrets

❧ To avoid a watery salsa, use only the outer flesh of the tomato.

❧ Be sure not to spill or splatter pomegranate juice on your clothing—it's one of the most difficult stains to remove.

about the chefs: "We simply cook what we like to eat ourselves," says Susan Feniger. Luckily, Feniger and Mary Sue Milliken's palates are in perfect harmony with the rest of America's. Hosts of *Too Hot Tamales*, one of the most successful programs on the national Television Food Network, Mary Sue and Susan take a nouveau bent toward Mexican cuisine, sharing culinary techniques and distinctive recipes with their audience. Their novel approach comes as no surprise as these chefs have long viewed cooking with a highly creative slant.

The two began their culinary careers back in high school. Mary Sue later attended Washburne Trade School's chef program and then apprenticed at the Conrad Hilton Hotel kitchen in Chicago. Susan attended the Culinary Institute of America in Hyde Park, New York.

Their paths first crossed at Chicago's distinguished Le Perroquet—they were the first women ever to work in the prestigious kitchen under the direction of owner/operator Jovan Treboyevic. In time, they went their separate ways, only to meet again when both were planning work sabbaticals in Europe. They hooked up again in Paris. On a handshake, they vowed to one day work together in California. They kept their word, opening an eclectic, international-inspired restaurant called City Café in Los Angeles. The restaurant brought them national recognition, as does Border Grill, the restaurant they now run in Santa Monica. For inspiration, Susan and Mary Sue regularly visit the marketplaces of Mexico. The cuisine of their popular restaurant has been called "the most serious Mexican food in town."

on judy's kitchen: Mary Sue and Susan cook with such originality and joy, it was sheer pleasure to have them on *Judy's Kitchen*. Although today these chefs are relaxed and charming television show hosts, their stint on my program was their first experience on television. Their apple-filled Mexican bread pudding, Capirotada, would make a delicious Rosh Hashanah dessert.

menu

~ Green Corn Tamales with Fresh Tomato Salsa

~ Border Grill Skewered Salmon

~ Capirotada (Mexican Bread Pudding)

green corn tamales with fresh tomato salsa

Using fresh corn instead of corn masa dough for tamales is a perfect example of how Mary Sue and Susan favor fresh ingredients. Unlike most tamales, these can easily be prepared in a kosher kitchen.

10 ears of corn (see Note)

2 tablespoons unsalted butter

½ teaspoon salt

¼ teaspoon freshly ground white pepper

½ cup heavy cream

Pinch of sugar, if needed

½ teaspoon baking powder

½ cup hominy grits

1 cup sour cream

Fresh Tomato Salsa (recipe follows)

Remove the corn husks by trimming off both ends of the cobs; try to keep the husks whole. Place the largest husks in a large pot, cover with hot water, and soak while preparing the tamale dough. Drain on paper towels. Cut one of the corn husks into ½-inch-wide strips to tie the tamales and set aside.

If using fresh corn, work over a bowl, running the point of a sharp knife down the center of each row of corn kernels, then scraping with the dull side to remove the kernels. You should have about 3 cups.

Melt the butter in a large skillet over medium heat. Add the corn and its juices, salt, pepper, cream, and sugar (if needed, depending on the sweetness of the corn). Simmer until the mixture thickens and some of the juices have evaporated, about 5 minutes. Cool. Stir in the

baking powder and hominy grits, cover with plastic wrap, and refrigerate.

To assemble the tamales, overlap 2 or 3 husks and spread about 3 tablespoons of corn filling down the center. Fold over the sides of the husk and then the ends to enclose the filling completely. Tie with the strips of corn husk into a package. Repeat with the remaining filling and corn husks.

To cook the tamales, use a steamer or a pot fitted with a rack. Make a bed for the tamales with the remaining corn husks. Add the tamales, cover, and steam over low heat for 1 hour. Remove the tamales and let rest for 10 minutes before serving.

To serve, arrange the hot tamales on a large platter or individual plates with sour cream and salsa.

Serves 6   Dairy

Note: If fresh corn is unavailable, substitute 3 cups canned corn kernels (not creamed) and chop in a food processor. In place of the fresh corn husks, buy dried corn husks and reconstitute them, or use parchment paper.

fresh tomato salsa

4 ripe tomatoes

1 to 2 jalapeño chilies, stemmed, seeded, and diced

1 cup chopped cilantro leaves

1 small red onion, finely diced

2 tablespoons fresh lime or lemon juice

Salt and freshly ground black pepper, to taste

Cut the tomatoes in half crosswise and remove the seeds. Cut into ¼-inch dice.

Combine the tomatoes, jalapeños, cilantro, onion, lime juice, salt, and pepper. Stir and toss well. Cover with plastic wrap and refrigerate no more than 1 day.

Makes 2 cups Pareve

border grill skewered salmon

This is one of Border Grill's signature dishes. The salmon is marinated in a flavorful Yucatán-style marinade, grilled or broiled, and served on a bed of steamed red chard.

1 salmon fillet (1½ pounds)

Bamboo skewers, 8 to 10 inches long, soaked in water

Salt and freshly ground black pepper, to taste

Yucatán-Style Marinade (recipe follows)

2 pounds red chard leaves, stemmed and torn into pieces

Lime Vinaigrette (recipe follows)

Cut the salmon into 1½-inch chunks and thread 4 to 5 chunks on each skewer. Sprinkle with salt and pepper and place in a shallow dish. Pour the marinade over the salmon and marinate for no longer than 20 to 30 minutes, turning to coat.

Preheat the grill or broiler.

Grill or broil the skewers about 1½ minutes per side. Or sauté the salmon in a hot nonstick skillet over high heat for 2 to 3 minutes per side, or until the fish is just cooked but still a little pink inside.

Bring a large pot of salted water to a boil over high heat and blanch the chard just until wilted.

Drain, transfer to a bowl of ice water, and drain again. Squeeze out any excess water. Transfer to a large bowl and toss with the vinaigrette.

To serve, place the chard leaves on plates and arrange the skewered salmon on top.

Serves 6 Pareve

yucatán-style marinade

3 ounces achiote paste (see Note)

1 cup fresh orange juice

¾ cup fresh lime juice

8 garlic cloves, roughly chopped

1½ tablespoons freshly cracked peppercorns

2½ cups finely chopped cilantro

Place the achiote, orange juice, lime juice, garlic, and peppercorns in a blender and blend well. Add the cilantro and blend again. Cover with plastic wrap and refrigerate for not more than 3 days.

Makes 3 to 4 cups Pareve

Note: Achiote paste is a bright orange seasoning paste consisting of annatto seeds, oregano, cumin, cinnamon, pepper, and cloves. It is often thinned with lemon juice for marinades and sauces. It is sold in bricks in Mexican markets, but you can simply season the marinade with the same spices.

lime vinaigrette

1   small shallot, minced

½   cup olive oil

2   tablespoons fresh lime juice

Salt and freshly ground black pepper, to taste

Place the shallot, olive oil, and lime juice in a small bowl and mix well. Season with salt and pepper. Cover with plastic wrap and refrigerate for up to 2 days.

Makes about ¾ cup   Pareve

capirotada (mexican bread pudding)

This bread pudding is designed to use up bread that is no longer fresh. The brown sugar, cinnamon, and apples make it a perfect Rosh Hashanah dessert. For Passover, replace the bread with Passover sponge cake.

8   tablespoons (1 stick) unsalted butter

½   loaf French bread, with crust, cut into cubes

1   pound brown sugar

1½ teaspoons ground cinnamon

2   large Granny Smith apples, peeled, cored, and chopped

1   cup walnuts, toasted and chopped (see page 165)

8   ounces cream cheese, chilled and crumbled

1   cup crème fraîche (see page 165), sour cream, or whipped cream, for garnish

Preheat the oven to 350°F.

Melt the butter in a medium saucepan, add the bread cubes, and stir to coat evenly. Spread the cubes on a baking sheet and bake for 15 minutes, or until lightly brown and crisp. Remove the bread and turn the oven temperature up to 400°F.

Combine 1½ cups water and the brown sugar in a heavy saucepan over medium-high heat and bring to a boil. Remove from heat. Stir in the cinnamon and set aside.

Combine the apples, walnuts, cream cheese, and toasted bread cubes in a large bowl. Drizzle the reserved brown sugar syrup over the bread mixture and mix thoroughly. Spoon into a well-buttered 13 x 9-inch glass casserole.

Bake, uncovered, stirring occasionally, for 15 minutes. Bake for 5 minutes more, without stirring, until the top is golden brown and crusty and the liquid is almost completely absorbed.

To serve, spoon warm bread pudding on serving plates with crème fraîche, sour cream, or whipped cream.

Serves 8 to 10   Dairy

chef's secrets

❧ To juice a lemon, first roll it on a firm surface to soften it. Cut the lemon crosswise in half, insert a fork, and twist it to release the juices while squeezing.

❧ Susan prefers to chop onions by hand. A food processor releases the juices from the onion, turning it yellow and bringing out the bitterness.

❧ To mash garlic, chop the garlic on a work surface, add a little salt, and use the flat side of a knife to mash the garlic.

MICHAEL McCARTY

california cuisine pioneer

about the chef: Who gets the credit for creating contemporary California cuisine? Naturally, no one chef devised this American regional cooking style. But when mentioning such names as Michael Roberts and Alice Waters, many feel compelled to include Michael McCarty as well.

Michael was only twenty-five years old when he opened Michael's in Santa Monica in 1979. Guests were wowed by his food's sophistication. The quality of ingredients was unsurpassed, and the presentations were restrained and elegant and dramatic—all at the same time. Michael's also became a hotbed for talent. So many now-famous chefs have worked in this legendary kitchen, it would take too long to list them. Michael's still runs smoothly, adapting to the 1990s as well as it did to the decade before. The cuisine tastes lighter; the use of butter and cream is more restrained. Michael published *Michael's Cookbook*, his first cookbook, and has opened a second namesake restaurant in New York City. This establishment is yet another Michael McCarty success story.

How did someone so young pull off something so great? Besides possessing confidence, Michael had impressive credentials. Most of his education was in France at the École Hôtelier de Paris, the Cordon Bleu, and the Academie du Vin. Once his culinary education was complete, Michael and a couple of friends opened Xavier, a Paris restaurant featuring an American slant on French cuisine. In 1975, Michael returned to the United States and earned a bachelor's degree in the Business and Art of Gastronomy from the University of Colorado. Michael now lives with his wife and children in Malibu, where they cultivate a hillside of grapevines and make their own wine.

on judy's kitchen: Michael was witty, charming, and provocative, very focused on where food should be in the 1990s. He emphasized that what we eat today should be a combination of the freshest ingredients and the simplest presentation. He plans his menus around the best seasonal ingredients available in local farmers' markets. Michael presented the Warm Wild Mushroom Salad and the Grilled Salmon with Baby Vegetables and Tomato Concassé on oversized white plates—just as he does at the restaurant. By using neutral chinaware, he ensures that the food remains the star and that its bright colors literally jump off the plate.

menu

~ Warm Wild Mushroom Salad

~ Grilled Salmon with Baby Vegetables and Tomato Concassé

~ Mixed Berry Gratin

warm wild mushroom salad

Michael always seeks a contrast of flavor and texture when creating a salad. Here he combines mâche, baby limestone lettuce, radicchio, and arugula. The latter adds a hint of spice to the mixture. The tasty vinaigrette with wild mushrooms also doubles as a sauce for grilled, roasted, or barbecued chicken, or sweetbreads. Michael suggests you have all the ingredients measured and prepared in advance, then assemble the salad just before serving.

6   cups assorted baby greens, such as mâche, arugula, limestone lettuce, and radicchio

¼   cup walnut oil

¼   cup pine nuts

2   large shallots, finely chopped

2   garlic cloves, finely chopped

½   pound *each* fresh chanterelle, shiitake, and oyster mushrooms, trimmed and cut into ½-inch pieces

¼   cup sherry wine vinegar

2   tablespoons *each* minced basil, tarragon, thyme, and chives

Salt and freshly ground white pepper, to taste

Tear up the salad greens and place them in a large salad bowl, tossing lightly.

Heat the walnut oil in a large skillet just until it begins to smoke. Add the pine nuts and sauté until toasted, about 30 seconds. Add the shallots, stirring quickly, then add the garlic and sauté until golden, about 30 seconds. Watch carefully so that it doesn't burn. Add the mushrooms and sear, without stirring, for 30 seconds, or until nicely browned. Do not overcook. Add the vinegar, stirring and scraping to deglaze the pan. Stir in the herbs, salt, and pepper.

To serve, pour the hot dressing over the salad and gently toss to coat all the greens. Mound the mixture on salad plates, making sure the mushrooms are evenly distributed. Serve immediately.

Serves 6   Pareve

grilled salmon with baby vegetables and tomato concassé

Fillet of sole was once the fish du jour of upscale restaurants. Today, salmon seems to be the hands-down favorite. Buy the freshest fish you can find; the salmon should be a deep coral color. Be careful not to overcook so it maintains its rich, moist taste.

Blanching and then sautéing baby vegetables in butter enhances their delicate flavor. If you can't find such gourmet produce in your market, substitute the smallest and freshest vegetables available. (For a light lunch, you could serve the salmon with salad greens instead of baby vegetables.) The tomato concassé, a coarsely chopped raw tomato mixture, replaces a more traditional sauce for a lighter dish.

6   *each* assorted baby vegetables, such as fresh baby corn, baby beets, baby white turnips, baby carrots, zucchini, butternut squash, haricots verts

4   tablespoons (½ stick) unsalted butter, melted

6   salmon fillets (6 ounces each), skinned, with small bones removed with tweezers

Salt and freshly ground white pepper, to taste

Tomato Concassé (recipe follows)

Blanch the vegetables in a large pot of boiling water for 1 minute. Heat 2 tablespoons butter in a nonstick skillet over medium heat and sauté the vegetables until coated with butter and tender, about 5 minutes.

Preheat the grill or broiler until very hot.

Brush the salmon fillets with the remaining butter and season with salt and pepper. Grill the fish until medium-rare and still red in the center, 4 to 5 minutes per side. If you prefer, grill until cooked through. While grilling, rotate the fillets 90 degrees to give them crosshatch grill marks on both sides.

To serve, place each fillet on 1 side of a heated large plate. Arrange the baby vegetables in a fan shape opposite the salmon. Spoon the Tomato Concassé on the other side of the salmon.

Serves 6   Dairy

tomato concassé

4   medium Roma tomatoes, peeled, seeded, and cut into ¼-inch dice (see page 166)

1   cup extra virgin olive oil

¼   cup balsamic vinegar (see Note)

½   medium shallot, finely chopped

2   tablespoons julienned basil leaves

Salt and freshly ground white pepper, to taste

Combine the tomatoes, olive oil, vinegar, shallot, and basil in a medium bowl. Season with salt and pepper and stir well. Cover with plastic wrap and marinate in the refrigerator for at least 15 minutes or up to 2 hours.

Makes 3 cups   Pareve

Note: For a kosher balsamic-style vinaigrette, see page 166.

mixed berry gratin

Everyone loves berries, and they're available year-round. They are plentiful throughout the United States in the late spring and flown in from places like Australia and Chile in the colder months. In the summer, try using peaches, and instead of framboise, flavor the custard with a peach-flavored liqueur.

1¾   cups Crème Anglaise (recipe follows)

4½   cups fresh berries, such as raspberries, strawberries, blackberries, or blueberries

¾   cup sugar

¾   cup framboise or sweet Concord grape wine, or to taste

2   cups heavy cream, lightly whipped just until thickened

¾   cup sliced almonds

Prepare the Crème Anglaise.

Preheat the broiler until very hot.

Gently toss the berries with the framboise and ¼ cup of the sugar in a mixing bowl. Arrange the berries in six 8-ounce gratin dishes or shallow ovenproof bowls, reserving the juice.

Fold the whipped cream and ¼ cup of the remaining framboise mixture into the Crème Anglaise. Pour this mixture over the berries.

Sprinkle each serving with the sliced almonds and the remaining sugar. Place the gratin dishes on a baking sheet and place under the broiler until the surface of the cream is browned and bubbly, about 20 seconds.

To serve, place each gratin dish on a plate and serve immediately.

Serves 6   Dairy

crème anglaise

2   cups milk

1   vanilla bean

4   large egg yolks

½   cup sugar

1   teaspoon grated orange zest

Bring the milk to a boil in a medium saucepan over medium-high heat, stirring frequently to prevent scorching. Remove the saucepan from the heat. Using a sharp knife, cut the vanilla bean lengthwise and scrape out the seeds. Add to the milk and let infuse for 5 minutes.

Using a wire whisk, beat the egg yolks, sugar, and orange zest in a medium bowl until the mixture turns creamy and light yellow in color, about 2 minutes. Whisking constantly, slowly pour in the milk mixture. Return the mixture to the saucepan and cook over low heat, stirring constantly, until thick enough to coat the back of a wooden spoon, about 1 minute.

Pour the Crème Anglaise through a fine-mesh strainer into a medium bowl. Let cool to room temperature. Cover and refrigerate. (This custard will keep up to 1 week, refrigerated.) Whisk any skin that forms on the surface back into the Crème Anglaise before using.

Makes about 2 cups   Dairy

chef's secrets

🌿 Unlike many chefs, Michael prefers white pepper for cooking. He feels it is less obtrusive in color and flavor than black pepper.

🌿 Continually taste food as you cook it, to achieve the correct balance of seasoning.

🌿 Plan presentation in advance, so you know how the food will appear on a plate before entertaining.

🌿 Handle salad greens carefully. Michael tears the leaves rather then cutting them with a knife, so they never looked crushed or bruised.

PHILIPPE JEANTY
napa valley's champagne chef

about the chef: Philippe Jeanty opened Domaine Chandon Winery Restaurant, one of the first trendy French restaurants in Napa Valley, and has been the chef there for more than twenty years. A native of France, Philippe was invited to join the restaurant staff when Chandon winery opened. With his mentor, Chef Joseph Thuet of Moët & Chandon, he traveled to Napa Valley for opening festivities. Jeanty stayed on to become chef.

Philippe became interested in cooking at the age of twelve. As a fourteen-year-old apprentice in Chef Thuet's kitchen at Moët, in Epernay, young Jeanty learned the fine points of French cuisine, including the delicate art of making Champagne sauces. His training then continued with Monsieur Ogier, at the esteemed Maîtres Cuisinières de France and at the Hotel and Restaurant School of Reims.

Jeanty relies on his palate, not recipes. He is convinced that each fish, apple—or even bottle of Champagne—is just different enough from any other that recipes must always be adjusted to taste.

on judy's kitchen: With blazing red hair and a fair complexion, Philippe, wearing his usual sweet smile, arrived at Los Angeles International Airport. I went to meet him. He brought a large crate filled with all the basic ingredients he needed. He hadn't forgotten a thing! When we arrived on the kitchen set, we needed only to fill bowls with the premeasured ingredients and arrange them in the correct order for each recipe. His style of food was designed to complement Napa Valley sparkling wine.

At Domaine Chandon, every holiday and special occasion is reason for a party. Philippe talked about one event in particular—a Fourth of July barbecue menu of steaks, mashed potatoes, and whole caramelized onions. Diced, those onions become a part of his savory tarte tatin.

When this busy chef is not cooking at Domaine Chandon, he operates a wholesale company supplying his own smoked salmon for other restaurants, delis, and private homes. Good friends for many years, we enjoyed working together. And, of course, we celebrated a successful show with a glass of his chilled sparkling wine.

menu

~ Caramelized Onion Tarte Tatin with Black Olive and Feta Vinaigrette

~ Crispy Salmon with a Parsley Salad and Roasted Vegetables with Garlic-Shallot Vinaigrette

~ Polenta Pudding with Berry Compote

caramelized onion tarte tatin with black olive and feta vinaigrette

When caramelized roasted onions and sautéed leeks are layered and enclosed in puff pastry, the result is a savory upside-down tart similar to the famous French apple tarte tatin.

Puff pastry, fresh or frozen and thawed in the refrigerator overnight

6 medium red onions, peeled

½ cup balsamic vinegar (see Note)

1 tablespoon olive oil

Kosher salt and freshly ground black pepper, to taste

Sautéed Leeks (recipe follows)

1 egg, lightly beaten

6 tablespoons crumbled feta

Black Olive and Feta Vinaigrette (recipe follows)

Cracked pepper, for garnish

6 sprigs chervil, for garnish

Roll out the puff pastry and cut it into six 4 ½-inch rounds. Cover with wax paper and refrigerate.

Preheat the oven to 350°F.

Place the onions in an 8-inch square baking dish. Pour the balsamic vinegar over them and drizzle with olive oil. Sprinkle with salt and pepper. Cover with foil and bake for 1 hour, or until cooked through, turning the onions over from time to time as they roast. Uncover and continue to bake for 15 minutes more. Set aside to cool and then dice.

Preheat the oven to 475°F.

Line the bottoms of six 4-inch tart pans with parchment paper cut into 4-inch circles. Spoon in a ½-inch layer of onions, then a ½-inch layer of leeks, packing them tightly. Cover each pan with a puff pastry round and brush with beaten egg. Place on a baking sheet and bake for 6 minutes, or until the pastry is golden brown.

To serve, invert each tart onto a plate and remove the tart pan, so that the pastry is on the bottom and the onion filling on top. Top each tart with 1 tablespoon feta cheese, add a dash of cracked pepper, and garnish with a sprig of chervil. Drizzle the vinaigrette around the tarts.

Serves 6   Dairy

Note: For a kosher balsamic-style vinegar, see page 166.

sautéed leeks

2 tablespoons unsalted butter

3 tablespoons olive oil

3 sprigs sage

3 sprigs thyme

4 medium leeks, white and light green parts, cut in half lengthwise, cleaned, and thinly sliced

Salt and freshly ground black pepper, to taste

Heat the butter and olive oil in a medium skillet over medium heat and sauté the sage and thyme for 1 minute. Add the leeks, salt, and pepper and sauté slowly until the leeks are tender, about 10 to 15 minutes, stirring occasionally. Set aside.

Makes about 2 cups   Dairy

black olive and feta vinaigrette

2½ tablespoons minced shallots

¼ cup oil-cured black olives, pitted and coarsely chopped

2 tablespoons cider vinegar

1 tablespoon sherry vinegar

¼ cup olive oil

¼ cup extra virgin olive oil

¼ cup crumbled feta

Salt and freshly ground black pepper, to taste

Whisk together the shallots, olives, vinegars, olive oils, and feta in a medium bowl. Season with salt and pepper.

Makes about 1 cup   Dairy

crispy salmon with a parsley salad and roasted vegetables with garlic-shallot vinaigrette

Philippe often uses parsley as a salad green, not just as a herb or garnish. He cooks the vegetables separately, since cooking times vary greatly. If you can't find really small potatoes, beets, and turnips, cut large ones in half. As Philippe arranged the salmon and vegetables on the serving dish, he described this entree as "a summer garden on a plate." How true.

3 cups fresh Italian flat-leaf parsley, stems removed

18 baby beets, scrubbed, tops off

⅓ cup olive oil

Salt and freshly ground black pepper, to taste

30 tiny yellow or red potatoes, scrubbed

Fresh thyme, to taste

Fresh sage, to taste

4 tablespoons (½ stick) unsalted butter

18 baby turnips, scrubbed

1 cup Vegetable Stock (page 166)

18 baby carrots, scrubbed

1 teaspoon caraway seeds

½ pound yellow wax beans, cut into pieces

6 salmon fillets (6 ounces each), skin on

Garlic-Shallot Vinaigrette (recipe follows)

Preheat the oven to 350°F. Line a baking sheet with foil.

Wash the parsley, discarding any damaged leaves. Dry and set aside.

Toss the beets in 1½ tablespoons of the olive oil in a medium bowl. Season with salt and pepper. Transfer to a small roasting pan and bake for 30 minutes, or until tender. Peel and set aside.

Wash and dry the potatoes. Place in a medium bowl and toss in 1½ tablespoons of the olive oil. Season with salt, pepper, thyme, and sage. Transfer to the baking sheet and bake for 30 minutes, or until tender. Set aside.

Heat 1½ tablespoons of the butter in a nonstick skillet over low heat. Add the turnips and toss to coat. Sauté until tender, adding a little stock if needed, about 10 minutes. Set aside.

Heat 1½ tablespoons of the remaining butter in a nonstick skillet over low heat. Add the carrots, salt, pepper, and caraway seeds and toss to coat. Cook, partially covered, until tender, about 10 minutes. Add a little stock occasionally to prevent sticking or burning. Set aside.

Heat the remaining butter in a nonstick skillet over medium heat and sauté the beans until tender, about 10 minutes.

Preheat the oven to 375°F.

Heat 2 tablespoons of the remaining olive oil in a nonstick ovenproof skillet over medium heat and brown the salmon, skin side down, for 2 minutes, or until the skin is crisp and develops a little color. (The salmon can be prepared ahead to this point.) Transfer the skillet to the preheated oven and finish cooking for 5 to 10 minutes, or until the skin is charred and fish is just cooked through.

To serve, arrange a salmon fillet on each plate, arrange the parsley around the salmon, and top with vegetables. Drizzle with the vinaigrette.

Serves 6   Dairy

garlic-shallot vinaigrette

2   garlic cloves, chopped

3   shallots, chopped

¼   cup red wine vinegar

1   tablespoon sherry vinegar

1   cup olive oil

Salt and freshly ground black pepper, to taste

Whisk together the garlic, shallots, vinegars, and olive oil in a small bowl. Season with salt and pepper. Set aside in a warm place for about 30 minutes to infuse the flavors.

Makes about 1½ cups   Pareve

polenta pudding with berry compote

Philippe acknowledged that the polenta and mascarpone are very Italian. But with a quick grin, he quipped, "Everyone knows that the French taught the Italians everything they know about cooking!"

Berry Compote (recipe follows)

¾   pound (3 sticks) unsalted butter, softened

5   cups confectioners' sugar

1   teaspoon vanilla extract

4   large eggs

2   large egg yolks

2   cups unbleached all-purpose flour

1   cup polenta

Mascarpone Cream (recipe follows)

12   mint leaves, for garnish

Prepare the Berry Compote and set aside.

Preheat the oven to 325°F. Grease and flour a 12-inch round cake pan.

Beat the butter, sugar, and vanilla in the bowl of an electric mixer until creamy. Beat in the eggs and the yolks, one at a time. Using a rubber spatula, fold in the flour and polenta. Pour into the cake pan and bake for 45 minutes, or until a toothpick inserted into the center comes out clean. Unmold onto a rack and cool.

Cut the cake into 12 wedges and place in a large shallow baking dish. Pour the Berry Compote with its juices on top of and around the cake wedges. Cover and refrigerate for 24 hours, basting the cake with compote occasionally.

Prepare the Mascarpone Cream and set aside.

To serve, place individual portions on dessert plates and spoon Mascarpone Cream on top. Garnish with the reserved berries. Add a mint leaf, and spoon some of the berry juices around the pudding.

Serves 12   Dairy

berry compote

3   quarts mixed fresh berries, such as blackberries, blueberries, raspberries, or strawberries

½   cup sugar, or to taste, depending on ripeness of fruit

Reserve 1 cup of the berries for garnish. Place the remaining berries and sugar in a heavy saucepan and carefully combine with a wooden spoon. Bring to a slow boil over medium-low heat and simmer for 20 minutes. Set aside.

Makes about 3 cups   Pareve

mascarpone cream

½   cup mascarpone, yogurt, or heavy cream

1   cup heavy cream, whipped to soft peaks

1½ tablespoons sugar

Stir the mascarpone in a large bowl and fold in the whipped cream and sugar.

Makes about 2 cups   Dairy

IN BOTH CONTEMPORARY and old-style Jewish cookery, poultry or meat usually takes on the star role in a meal. I often think of my mother's Friday night shabbat dinners that showcased chicken in all its glory—chicken fricassee to start, followed by chicken soup with matzo balls, and roast chicken with potato kugel. My mother wasn't a great cook, but she cooked from her heart. And she cooked what she knew, which was what her mother had taught her. ❧ While I have great fondness for these handed-down recipes so typical of many Jewish households, I tend to prepare poultry and meat in a different way today. And I often turn to the recipes in this chapter for inspiration. For instance, I regularly prepare Michael Frank's and Robert Bell's Chicken Breasts with Prune Stuffing. There's something about this flavor combination that's irresistible. And the Oven-braised Veal Shanks created by Patrick Healy are too melt-in-your-mouth to pass up. If I ever feel blue, I turn to Hans Röckenwagner's Beef Goulash. One mouthful of this comforting stew and I've just got to smile. ❧ With this book, feel free to get creative. Please don't think you are restricted to preparing an entire menu from one chef. One chef's entrees can be paired with appetizers and desserts from other chefs. To inspire your experimentation, I've created a couple of sample menus that combine recipes from different chefs. ❧ SUNDAY BUFFET BRUNCH: *José's Jícama Slaw, Moroccan Tomato Salad, Turkey Sausage with Fruit Liqueur, Pommes Seder (Oven-fried Potatoes), Roasted Asparagus, Banana-Rum and Lemon-Lime Ices* ❧ A MEMORABLE MAKE-AHEAD FOUR-COURSE DINNER: *Chopped Chicken Livers on Crostini, Roasted Eggplant Soup with Red Pepper Puree, Crusty Rosemary Rolls, Short Rib Terrine with Herb Vinaigrette and Fruit Ices*

about the chefs: Michael Franks comes from a long line of restaurateurs, representing the third generation in his family to follow the tradition. Born in London of Jewish parents, he trained at such well-known London luxury hotels as the Dorchester, the Savoy, and Grosvenor House. In 1976, Michael moved to Los Angeles to run a group of restaurants. There, he teamed up with Robert Bell.

Robert Bell grew up in New York, where his father worked in restaurants most of his life. He loved to assist his father and became fascinated with the culinary profession at a young age. The family moved to California, and while attending Hollywood High School, Robert became interested in architecture. After graduating, he worked in that field for fifteen years. Realizing that his real love was cooking, he started working at Courtney's Restaurant, where he met Michael Franks.

Together, Michael and Robert opened Chez Mélange and during the next ten years opened four other restaurants: Chez Allez, Fino, Misto Café/Bakery, and Depot. Recently they opened The Chez restaurant in the Beverly Prescott Hotel in Los Angeles. The pair has won many honors and awards, including Chez Mélange's designation as a Gold Star Restaurant by the *Los Angeles Times*. In 1990, they received the California Restaurant Writers Association's Restaurateurs of the Year award.

on judy's kitchen: Michael and Robert prepared an unusual Passover menu with an English accent. Michael explained that although most of the food on his family's seder plate was traditional, his mother disliked lamb so much that she replaced it with a chicken bone. Rabbis now agree that vegetarian Jews can substitute a roasted beet for the lamb shank.

Michael and Robert's teamwork really paid off. Michael prepared a recipe for Fried Gefilte Fish with Horseradish Aïoli—just like his mother made when he was growing up in London. Despite the pressure on the set, they created such an outstanding Passover menu, I have included some of their dishes at our family seders.

menu

~ Fried Gefilte Fish with Horseradish Aïoli

~ Chicken Breasts with Prune Stuffing

~ Pommes Seder (Oven-fried Potatoes)

~ Roasted Asparagus

~ Mum's English Matzo Pudding

fried gefilte fish with horseradish aïoli

Michael serves this as a California-style warm salad, topped with a horseradish aïoli sauce.

1½   pounds salmon fillet

1½   pounds whitefish

3   carrots, diced

1   onion, diced

5   eggs

2   cups matzo meal

Salt and freshly ground black pepper, to taste

½   cup safflower oil

4   cups assorted lettuce greens, tossed in oil

Horseradish Aïoli (recipe follows)

Grind the salmon, whitefish, carrots, and onion in a grinder or food processor. Place the ground mixture in a large bowl and blend with 3 eggs and 1 cup of the matzo meal. Season with salt and pepper. The mixture should be soft and light to the touch.

Place the remaining 1 cup matzo meal in a shallow bowl. Moisten your hands with oil and shape the fish mixture into cakes or patties. Beat the remaining 2 eggs in a shallow bowl and carefully dip each cake into the beaten eggs, then into the matzo meal, coating completely.

Heat the oil in a large heavy frying pan over medium-high heat and fry the patties until golden brown on each side.

To serve, arrange the greens on plates, top with warm gefilte fish patties, and aïoli.

Makes about 24 fish cakes   Pareve

horseradish aïoli

4   garlic cloves, pounded or crushed to a paste

3   egg yolks

Juice of ½ lemon

Salt, to taste

2   cups olive oil

1   tablespoon prepared red horseradish

All ingredients must be at room temperature.

Blend the garlic, egg yolks, lemon juice, and salt, in a food processor until the consistency of a thick, sticky paste. With the motor running, gradually pour in the oil in a thin stream. The mixture should turn the consistency of thick mayonnaise. Carefully mix in the horseradish. Transfer to a small bowl, cover with plastic wrap, and refrigerate.

Makes about 3 cups   Pareve

chicken breasts with prune stuffing

These Moroccan-style chicken breasts are different from any I have ever tasted. The special flavor comes from the stuffing of prunes and curry powder, combined with vegetables and crumbled matzo. This Passover entree has the taste of the *tzimmes* that my mother made during the holiday.

1   cup pitted dried prunes

¼   cup olive oil

2   tablespoons chopped garlic

¼   cup diced onion

¼   cup diced celery

¼ cup diced carrots

1 teaspoon curry powder

1 teaspoon ground cardamom

2 whole matzos, crumbled

1 egg

Salt and freshly ground black pepper, to taste

4 whole chicken breasts, skin on, boned and cut in half

8 lemon wedges

Place the prunes in a small saucepan and add water to cover. Bring to a boil over high heat, reduce heat, and simmer until soft, about 10 minutes. Drain and dice. Set aside.

Preheat the oven to 375°F. Line a baking sheet with foil.

To prepare the stuffing, heat the oil in a large skillet over medium heat and sauté the garlic, onion, celery, carrots, prunes, curry powder, and cardamon. Let cool. Add the matzo and egg. Season with salt and pepper.

Place a chicken breast, skin side down, on a work surface and spoon stuffing in the center. Roll up the chicken breast, encasing the stuffing, and tie with string. Place on the baking sheet. Brush with oil and season with salt and pepper. Repeat with the remaining chicken breasts.

Bake for 20 minutes, then increase the heat to 425°F. Bake about 5 minutes more, or until the chicken is tender and crisp. Transfer to a cutting board and slice on the bias, using an electric knife if possible.

To serve, arrange sliced chicken breasts on plates with lemon wedges.

Serves 8   Meat

pommes seder (oven-fried potatoes)

4 russet potatoes, scrubbed and thinly sliced

8 tablespoons (1 stick) unsalted margarine, melted

Salt and freshly ground black pepper, to taste

Preheat the oven to 375°F. Oil a baking sheet.

Brush a nonstick skillet with margarine and arrange the potatoes in a ring, overlapping. Pour margarine over the potato slices until completed coated. Sauté over high heat until golden brown. Using a metal spatula, carefully transfer to the baking sheet. Repeat with the remaining potato slices. Bake for 15 minutes, or until crisp.

Serves 8   Pareve

roasted asparagus

2 pounds asparagus

8 tablespoons (1 stick) unsalted margarine, melted

Salt and freshly ground black pepper, to taste

Preheat the oven to 350°F. Line a baking sheet with foil.

Cut off the ends of the asparagus and, using a potato peeler, peel off any fiber around the ends. Brush with margarine and place on the baking sheet. Sprinkle with salt and pepper.

Bake for about 15 minutes, or until tender.

Serves 8   Pareve

mum's english matzo pudding

Matzo goes Cordon Bleu! For Passover, matzo replaces the usual noodles in this dessert kugel.

2	tablespoons unsalted margarine, melted, for baking dish
½	cup ground almonds, for baking dish
4½	whole matzos
½	cup apple juice
3	eggs, lightly beaten
½	cup sugar
½	cup golden raisins
½	cup diced dried apricots
1	cup whole unblanched almonds
½	cup sliced almonds
½	teaspoon ground cinnamon
1	tablespoon fresh orange juice
8	tablespoons (1 stick) unsalted margarine, melted

Preheat the oven to 350°F. Generously grease an 8-inch square baking dish and dust with ground almonds.

Coarsely crumble the matzo in a large bowl and add the apple juice and beaten eggs. Add the sugar, raisins, apricots, whole and sliced almonds, cinnamon, orange juice, and margarine and mix well. Pour into the baking dish.

Bake for 40 to 50 minutes, or until firm and golden brown.

Serves 8   Pareve

chef's secrets

❦ How to know if you're buying fresh chicken: Call your butcher and find out what day he receives his shipment of fresh chickens. If you are in doubt as to freshness, buy frozen chicken.

❦ When sautéing or baking a chicken over high heat or at a high temperature, such as 425°F to 500°F, the chicken becomes crisp on the outside and tender and moist on the inside.

❦ When slicing cooked stuffed breasts on the bias, use an electric knife for cleaner, sharper slices.

a b o u t   t h e   c h e f : Think perfect pastries and it's impossible not to think of Michel Richard. This internationally acclaimed French chef first captured America's attention when he opened a Los Angeles *pâtisserie* in 1977. His divine desserts were the talk of the town. Even the most jaded dessert lovers gushed over the originality of his confections.

Ten years later, buoyed by public affection, Michel debuted Citrus, a California-French restaurant on Melrose Avenue in Hollywood. Success was instantaneous. His savory dishes were rated as high as his sweet ones. And if Michel's food didn't win patrons over, his personality did. Few guests could resist his warm smile and joie de vivre.

While Citrus remains Michel's home base, he has opened several other dining establishments, including the fashionable Citronelle restaurants in Santa Barbara, California, and Washington, D.C. He has also co-authored the best-selling *Michel Richard's Home Cooking with a French Accent*. Unlike many chef's cookbooks that are filled with difficult recipes and unusual ingredients, Michel's highlights simple but delicious dishes.

Michel loves to cook for family and friends, and Sunday is usually the day he's at his home stove. Michel built a backyard pizza oven, which he uses to barbecue whole fish, chicken or meat. His at-home meals are heartier—more country— than those he serves at his restaurants. They're often filled with the flavors of his native Brittany. Champagne, as bubbly as Michel's personality, is definitely on the menu.

o n   j u d y ' s   k i t c h e n : A close friend, Michel has often appeared on my show. He does get nervous when doing television, because he worries about his French accent. In fact, he's easy to understand, and his vitality and culinary artistry make him a colorful television personality. His enthusiasm is contagious. This man loves everything about his work. He may feel nervous on camera, yet he radiates unshakable confidence in his cooking.

Like many modern French chefs, Michel has learned to concentrate food flavor's through reduction and other techniques, instead of relying on butter and cream. That made it easy for him to create a kosher meat menu. Texture is a vital component of Michel's dishes and he's perpetually searching for new textural combinations. He jokes that he's so obsessed with texture, he's often called "Captain Crunch." Discovering such American staples as Rice Krispies and frozen corn tickles his classic French palate.

m e n u

~ Short Rib Terrine with Herb Vinaigrette

~ Caramelized Apple Napoleons

short rib terrine with herb vinaigrette

This terrine was named Best Recipe of the Year by the *Los Angeles Times*. Twelve pounds may seem like an enormous quantity of meat, but after the short ribs are baked, removed from the bone, and layered in a terrine, you'll see the amount is just right.

I sometimes serve this dish on a bed of greens to start our Shabbat dinner.

12 pounds large, meaty short ribs

Salt and freshly ground black pepper, to taste

3   medium onions, unpeeled and quartered

2   stalks celery, sliced

3   carrots, sliced

3   tomatoes, coarsely chopped

2   whole heads garlic, unpeeled, cut crosswise in half and cloves separated

2   bay leaves

10 sprigs thyme or 3 tablespoons dried thyme, crumbled

10 sprigs parsley

1   tablespoon crushed black peppercorns

2   quarts Chicken Stock (page 167)

Herb Vinaigrette (recipe follows)

Kosher salt, to taste

Preheat the oven to 350°F. Season the short ribs with salt and pepper. Place the ribs in a large roasting pan. Scatter the onions, celery, carrots, tomatoes, garlic, bay leaves, thyme, parsley, and peppercorns over them. Make a second layer of ribs if necessary. Pour in enough stock to cover the meat. Place the pan on the stovetop over medium-high heat and bring to a boil. Cover the pan tightly with aluminum foil and bake for 3 hours, or until the meat is very tender and falling off the bones.

Using a slotted spoon, remove the ribs from the broth while still warm. Reserve the broth and vegetables. Remove the bones, fat, and gristle, leaving the meaty portion in 1 large strip for the terrine, if possible.

To assemble the terrine, line a 9 x 5-inch loaf pan with plastic wrap, leaving an overhang of several inches. Pack the short ribs lengthwise into the pan with some of the cooked carrots as tightly as possible. Make several layers. Fold the plastic wrap over the loaf pan to cover. Place the terrine in a dish or tray to catch spilling juices. Place a second 9 x 5-inch loaf pan over the terrine to compress it. Tie the loaf pans together with string at each end. Pour off any juices. Refrigerate for at least 24 hours.

Strain the cooking broth through a fine-mesh sieve, pressing on the ingredients. Cover and refrigerate. Prepare the herb vinaigrette and chill.

To serve, remove the terrine from the refrigerator, cut the strings, and remove the top loaf pan. Open the plastic wrap and invert the terrine onto a cutting board. Immediately slice it into ½- to ¾-inch-thick slices, using a sharp knife and a broad spatula.

To serve cold, place each slice on a plate. Sprinkle lightly with kosher salt and ladle the vinaigrette alongside.

To serve warm, preheat the oven to 350°F. Place cold slices on individual ovenproof plates and reheat for 5 minutes. Remove the chilled layer of fat from the cooking broth.

Reheat and ladle several tablespoons of broth over each slice of meat. Sprinkle lightly with kosher salt. Ladle the vinaigrette alongside.

Serves 6 to 8   Meat

herb vinaigrette

¼ cup Dijon mustard

1 egg yolk, at room temperature (see Note)

½ cup red wine vinegar

1 cup olive oil

2 medium shallots, minced

¼ cup minced chives or green onions

½ cup minced Italian flat-leaf parsley

Salt and freshly ground black pepper, to taste

Combine the mustard and egg yolk in a food processor or blender. With the machine running, pour in the vinegar and then the oil in a slow, thin stream. Stir in the shallots, chives, and parsley with a spoon. Season with salt and pepper. Transfer to a small bowl, cover with plastic wrap, and refrigerate.

Makes about 1½ cups   Pareve

Note: Since raw egg yolks might contain salmonella, you may chose to omit the egg yolk from this recipe.

caramelized apple napoleons

Michel, who began his career as a pastry chef, created this unusual and innovative dessert. Apples flambéed with brandy are sandwiched between caramelized phyllo pastry and garnished with caramelized apple sauce.

6 sheets phyllo dough

8 tablespoons (1 stick) unsalted margarine, melted

1 cup sugar

Pommes Flambées (recipe follows)

Apple Sauce (recipe follows)

Preheat the oven to 350°F. Place twelve 4-inch tartlet pans on a baking sheet. Brush the inside of the pans with margarine and sprinkle lightly with sugar.

Working with 1 phyllo sheet at a time, lay it out flat, covering the remaining sheets with wax paper and a damp towel. Using a pastry brush, lightly brush the sheet with melted margarine and sprinkle with sugar. Cut the sheet in half crosswise. Turn each of the half sheets over, sugared side down, and crumple it to fit into the bottom of one of the tartlet pans, pressing down gently. Repeat with the remaining phyllo sheets. Bake for 15 minutes, or until golden brown. Unmold while still hot and place sugar side up on cooling racks.

To serve, place a baked pastry round, sugar side down, on an individual plate. Arrange about 8 flambéed apple slices, overlapping, on top of the pastry. Top with another round of baked pastry, sugar side up. Spoon apple sauce around the pastry. Repeat the process with the remaining pastry rounds, flambéed apples, and apple sauce and serve immediately.

Makes 6 napoleons   Pareve

pommes flambées
(flambéed apples)

8   tablespoons (1 stick) unsalted margarine

1   cup sugar

8   Granny Smith apples (2 pounds), peeled,
    cored, and sliced ½ inch thick

2   tablespoons apple brandy

Melt the margarine with the sugar in a heavy
skillet over medium heat mixing until the sugar
dissolves. Add the apples and sauté until they
are caramelized but still firm. Heat the brandy
in a ladle until hot but not boiling. Pour over
the apples, stand back, and light it with a
match. Transfer the apples to a baking sheet to
cool. Use for filling the napoleons and for the
apple sauce.

Serves 10   Pareve

apple sauce

1   cup Pommes Flambées

½   cup apple juice

⅛   teaspoon ground cinnamon

Combine the apples, apple juice, and cinnamon in a food processor or blender and puree.
Transfer to a pitcher or bowl and set aside.

Makes about 1½ cups   Pareve

PATRICK HEALY

an american success story via france

about the chef: Few American chefs possess the illustrious background of Patrick Healy. He trained for five years with France's master chefs in Michelin three-star restaurants such as Le Moulin de Mougins in Mougins, Michel Guérard in southwest France, and Restaurant Troisgros in Roanne. But perhaps his most impressive education came from a source far closer to home—his grandmother. Harriet Healy is quite the culinary legend; she wrote cookbooks, ran a culinary school, and calls Julia Child a longtime friend. Patrick's grandmother encouraged his interest in cooking when he was a child. She even held crepe-flipping contests. Patrick's fate may have been permanently sealed when Julia Child invited Patrick and his family to dinner with her at Roger Vergé's Le Moulin de Mougins.

This chef's formal training began at L'Academie de Cuisine near Washington, D.C. He worked for the prestigious catering firm Ridgewell's in Washington, where he prepared embassy and State Department dinners. Patrick shot to stardom at Le St. Germain restaurant in Los Angeles. He then became executive chef at Colette before opening Champagne, his own highly acclaimed French restaurant. Today he is executive chef of Xiomara, a French bistro in Pasadena, and of Oye!, an upscale nouveau Cuban restaurant in the back of Xiomara. He is also consulting chef at the trendy Buffalo Club in Los Angeles, where he cooks creative American food.

Patrick remains greatly influenced by his culinary adventures in France, particularly Nice. "Niçoise cuisine tastes richer than what you might expect in such a warm climate," he says. "Yet at the same time, it still tastes light. And I love how it adapts so many Italian dishes, like gnocchi and ravioli, into its cooking style."

on judy's kitchen: When Patrick strolled onto the set, I immediately wished I had worn high heels or had a box to stand on. I had forgotten that he's so tall—or maybe that I'm so petite!

Patrick is no stranger to kosher cooking; he often prepares Passover menus at his restaurants. This made it easy for him to relax.

Patrick likes to describe his food as "simple and straightforward." While his recipes are uncomplicated, the flavors are impeccable. Both his roasted eggplant soup and the oven-braised veal shanks are excellent dishes to make in advance; they just get better sitting overnight in the refrigerator.

menu

~ Roasted Eggplant Soup with Red Pepper Puree
~ Oven-braised Veal Shanks with Wild Mushrooms and Wild Rice

roasted eggplant soup with red pepper puree

This hearty soup is as thick as a stew, with a rich dark color from the unpeeled eggplant. Serve it with pumpernickel or crusty country bread and a salad and you've got a complete yet light meal. The soup freezes well too; just add a little wine or water when reheating to thin to the desired consistency and to prevent scorching.

2   large eggplants (1½ pounds each)

½   cup olive oil

Salt and freshly ground black pepper, to taste

2   large red bell peppers

1   large onion, thinly sliced

3   garlic cloves, minced

4   cups Vegetable Stock or Pareve Chicken Stock (pages 166 and 167)

¼   cup julienned basil leaves, for garnish

Preheat the oven to 400°F.

Wash the eggplants, cut off the stems, and cut in half lengthwise . Place on a baking sheet, cut side up. Brush generously with ¼ cup of the olive oil and sprinkle lightly with salt and pepper. Bake for 30 minutes, or until dark golden brown. Let cool. Cut unpeeled eggplant into large chunks.

While the eggplant is roasting, place the peppers on top of a gas burner or under the broiler and cook, turning frequently, until the skin is charred. Place in a plastic bag, close, and let stand for 10 minutes. Peel off the skin. Place the peppers in a bowl of cold water and any excess peel will slip off. Remove the stems and discard the seeds. Place the peppers in a food processor or blender and puree until smooth. Season with salt. Spoon into a squeeze bottle or pastry bag with a plain tip. Set aside.

Heat the remaining ¼ cup olive oil in a deep heavy pot over low heat and sauté the onion and garlic for 5 to 10 minutes, or until translucent. Add the eggplant and stock to cover. Simmer, covered, for 15 minutes. Transfer to a food processor or blender and puree. Season with salt and pepper. Pour back into the pot and reheat before serving.

To serve, ladle the soup into heated soup bowls. Pipe your own signature design with the red pepper puree on top of the soup and sprinkle with basil.

Serves 4 to 6   Pareve

oven-braised veal shanks with wild mushrooms and wild rice

The use of olive oil, garlic, wine, and herbs is typical of the cuisine of Provence. Be sure to cook the veal long enough for the meat to almost fall from the bone; you shouldn't need a knife to eat this dish.

4   veal shanks (8 ounces each), about 2 inches thick

Salt and freshly ground black pepper, to taste

¼   cup plus 1 tablespoon olive oil

2   tablespoons unsalted margarine

1   large onion, chopped

2   carrots, chopped

1   stalk celery, chopped

1   head garlic, cut in half

2   tablespoons tomato paste

2   sprigs thyme

2   bay leaves

1½ cups Madeira or sherry

1 cup dry white wine

6 cups brown veal stock or Chicken Stock
(page 167)

4 ounces dried morels or black trumpet mushrooms

4 ounces fresh shiitake mushrooms, stems
removed

4 ounces fresh oyster mushrooms

5 ripe tomatoes, peeled, seeded, and chopped
(see page 166)

Wild Rice (recipe follows)

8 ears of baby corn, blanched, for garnish

8 baby carrots, blanched, for garnish

2 tablespoons chopped chives, for garnish

Preheat the oven to 350°F.

Tie each shank tightly with string to keep it on the bone while cooking. Season with salt and pepper.

Heat ¼ cup of the olive oil and 1 tablespoon of the margarine in a large roasting pan over high heat and brown the shanks. Add the onion, carrots, celery, garlic, tomato paste, thyme, and bay leaves, mixing with a wooden spoon until lightly browned. Add the Madeira and white wine, bring to a boil, and simmer until reduced by half. Add the stock and bring to a boil. Cover and bake until tender, 2 ½ to 3 hours. Transfer the shanks to a large platter; remove the string and keep warm. Strain all the vegetables from the sauce and simmer until thick.

Soak the dried morels in warm water to cover for 15 minutes, or until soft. Strain the morels through cheesecloth, reserving the soaking liquid. Set aside.

Heat the remaining olive oil and margarine in a nonstick skillet over medium heat. Add the shiitake and oyster mushrooms, salt, and pepper and sauté for 1 minute. Add the morels and tomatoes and sauté until soft. Mix the mushroom mixture into the sauce with the reserved soaking liquid and simmer for 5 minutes.

To serve, arrange each shank with the open marrow bone up in the center of a heated plate. Spoon the Wild Rice on the side and garnish with the baby corn and carrots. Spoon the sauce generously over the shanks. Sprinkle with chives.

Serves 4   Meat

wild rice

1 cup wild rice, well washed

2¼ cups boiling water

1 teaspoon salt

⅓ cup olive oil, or more to taste

Combine the wild rice, boiling water, and salt in a large pot over high heat and return to a boil. Reduce the heat and simmer, covered, for 45 minutes, or until the rice is tender but not mushy. Drain and shake over the heat to dry the grains. Toss with olive oil.

Serves 4   Pareve

chef's secrets

❧ When buying eggplant, look for smooth, firm vegetables. The color should be uniform, without any discoloration or spots.

❧ Patrick likes to season lightly with salt and pepper after each major addition when cooking. When seasoning only at the end, the dish will just taste salty.

about the chef: Imagine German precision blended with French technique and California ingenuity, and you've just conjured up the cooking style of Hans Röckenwagner. This handsome blond chef mans the stove at Röckenwagner, his namesake Santa Monica restaurant.

The ultramodern complex, designed by architect Frank Gehry, delights a cross section of patrons, from international tourists to famous Hollywood faces. Tucked into a corner of the restaurant is Hans's bustling bakery, which displays his crisp-crusted whole-grain breads and oversized pretzels.

Hans attended culinary school in Germany and apprenticed in the Black Forest. He fine-tuned his skills at Zum Adler, a Michelin two-star restaurant near Basel, Switzerland, where he learned the nuances of both classic and nouvelle French cuisine. He then moved to Chicago to work at the legendary Le Perroquet restaurant. In 1984, he opened his own dining establishment in Los Angeles. He debuted the little eatery in Venice, but the restaurant became so fashionable, he moved to larger quarters in Santa Monica. While busy running Röckenwagner, Hans also consults for other restaurateurs and often appears on television programs.

on judy's kitchen: When we booked Hans on my show, we asked him to prepare country-style dishes from his native Germany rather than the more sophisticated fare he serves at Röckenwagner. At first he was reluctant, since such foods are not part of his regular menu. Once he began cooking on camera, however, he rapidly warmed up to the subject. He began reminiscing about his childhood. It seems that in the Röckenwagner household, dinner was truly a family affair. Each parent prepared a specialty; for example, his father cooked the goulash and his mother made the Spätzle. Even today, Hans often serves Spätzle as a side dish at his restaurant.

After being a guest on *Judy's Kitchen*, this chef was so enthusiastic about preparing rustic German cuisine that he started a new tradition at Röckenwagner. One night each week, he features *Stammtisch*, or communal table. Single diners or those who would like to meet new people join forces and dine on hearty German fare such as weisswurst with homemade pretzel rolls served with imported Bavarian wheat beer. This friendly concept is just one of the many inventive ideas Hans has come up with at Röckenwagner.

menu

~ Beef Goulash

~ Spätzle (Tiny Dumplings)

beef goulash

This goulash takes at least two hours to cook, even longer if you like your beef practically falling apart. Watch the goulash carefully, and stir when necessary, so that it doesn't burn; add stock as needed to keep the sauce from getting overly thick. Hans uses Tabasco in this dish and considers it a necessity in his cooking. Accompany the stew with Spätzle or mashed potatoes.

5   tablespoons vegetable oil

3   cups diced onions

3   garlic cloves, minced

2   pounds lean beef, cut into 1-inch cubes

4   tablespoons tomato paste

½   cup unbleached all-purpose flour

6   cups veal, Chicken Stock, or Vegetable Stock
    (pages 167 and 166)

2   bay leaves

1   teaspoon paprika

Tabasco sauce or cayenne pepper, to taste

Salt and freshly ground black pepper, to taste

3   red bell peppers, seeded and diced

Heat 2 tablespoons of the oil in a large heavy pot over medium heat and sauté the onions and garlic until soft, about 10 minutes. Transfer to a bowl. Heat 2 tablespoons of the remaining oil in the same pot over high heat and brown the meat. Add the onions to the browned meat and stir well with a wooden spoon. Add the tomato paste and mix well. Blend in the flour and cook, mixing constantly, until the flour browns a little, about 3 minutes. Gradually add 4 cups of the stock, bay leaves, paprika, Tabasco, salt, and pepper and mix well. Bring to a boil, reduce heat, and simmer,

uncovered, for 30 minutes, stirring occasionally. Cover and continue to simmer for 30 minutes more.

Heat the remaining oil in a skillet over medium heat and sauté the red peppers. Add them to the beef mixture. If you like the peppers crisp, add them later, about 10 minutes before serving. Continue to cook, stirring often and adding additional stock as needed, for 1 hour, or until the meat is tender. Remove and discard the bay leaves.

To serve, ladle into heated plates or shallow soup bowls.

Serves 8   Meat

spätzle (tiny dumplings)

Hans says there is nothing like homemade spätzle, which he compares to a "home-style rustic pasta dish." The consistency of spätzle dough is soft, just a little thicker than a batter.

For a side dish to serve with baked chicken or grilled meats, sauté the spätzle in margarine.

8   eggs

Pinch of salt

½   teaspoon freshly grated nutmeg

5   cups unbleached all-purpose flour

Whisk the eggs together with ½ cup water, salt, and nutmeg in a large bowl, blending with a whisk until frothy. Add the flour all at once and mix well, adding more water as needed to make a thick, rather lumpy, sticky batter. Using your hands, mix the dough until it is stretchy. Divide the dough into thirds and cut into spätzle using one of the methods described below.

Bring a large pot of salted water to a boil. Boil the spätzle until it is tender and rises to the top, about 3 minutes. Using a slotted spoon, transfer the spätzle to a large bowl. Chill in cold water to stop the cooking process. Drain, cover with a damp cloth, and refrigerate until ready to serve. Serve as soon as possible.

Serves 8   Pareve

three methods for cutting spätzle

❧ Using a spätzle cutter: Spoon the dough into the small container on top of the spätzle cutter. Sit the machine on top of the pot and push the container back and forth against the grate, allowing the spätzle to drop into the boiling water. Do not crowd the spätzle in the pot.

❧ Using a wooden board and knife: Place the dough on a small wooden board. Dip a knife in warm water and, holding the board over the boiling water, cut the dough, allowing small pieces to fall into the pot.

❧ Using a potato ricer: Fill a potato ricer with a spoonful of the dough, cover with the top, and push, allowing the dough to come through the small holes into the boiling water.

MICHEL OHAYON

kosher cuisine, moroccan style

about the chef: Michel Ohayon is one chef who is as at home in a kosher kitchen as he is in a restaurant kitchen, in this case at Koutoubia, his Moroccan restaurant. At the highly regarded West Los Angeles dining establishment, Michel creates food reflecting the French, Jewish, and Arab influences of his upbringing. Raised in Morocco, he learned to cook at the age of seven by following his grandmother around the kitchen.

When Michel was in his early twenties, he moved to the United States. His first American home was San Francisco, and then he came to Los Angeles. He worked at several local restaurants, beginning as a busboy and runner at the legendary Ma Maison before moving up to captain at Dar Maghreb, a lavish Moroccan restaurant in Hollywood. In 1976, Michel's career took a giant leap forward when he assisted in the opening of Marrakesh restaurant in Newport Beach, California. Two years later, he established Koutoubia.

on judy's kitchen: I can't think of a more exotic show than the one we taped at Koutoubia. Michel was dressed in a *galapa*, an embroidered ankle-length robe. We sat on a pillowed sofa in front of a copper tray table, sipping sweetened hot tea and nibbling almond-filled pastries as we chatted about Moroccan dishes served during the Jewish holidays. If you're looking for an unusual holiday menu, Michel's recipes would make a terrific

Moroccan-inspired Rosh Hashanah dinner, one that would not easily be forgotten. In fact, this is part of the menu Michel presented to his guests for lunch following the Bar Mitzvah of his son.

For the show, Michel prepared three Moroccan salads. These dishes are not salads as we know them, but more like Italian antipasti—spiced or sweetened vegetables presented on a large platter at the beginning of a meal to refresh the palate and spark the appetite. He also made bastilla, the classic Moroccan phyllo pie scented with cinnamon and filled with chicken, almonds, and scrambled eggs. Finally he prepared a hearty couscous with tender lamb.

Michel is much taken with the incredible variety of produce available year-round in California. "We have not only peppers and tomatoes like in the Mediterranean regions, but also carrots, squash, white and green asparagus—even our own truffles," he notes. "These vegetables are my constant source of inspiration."

menu

~ Morrocan Tomato Salad

~ Morrocan Beet Salad

~ Morrocan Carrot Salad

~ Lamb and Vegetable Couscous

moroccan tomato salad

Michel suggests using the heart of the celery for this salads because it is more tender than the outer stalks.

8   Roma tomatoes, peeled and diced (page 166)

2   tablespoons minced parsley

2   tablespoons minced cilantro

2   green onions, minced

½   cup diced green bell pepper

3   stalks celery, from the heart, diced

Salt and freshly ground black pepper, to taste

¼   cup olive oil

Juice of 1 lemon

Combine the tomatoes, parsley, cilantro, green onions, bell pepper, and celery in a large bowl. Season with salt and pepper. Toss with the olive oil and lemon juice until well combined.

Serves 8   Pareve

moroccan beet salad

Beets are often the forgotten vegetable. How often do you see them in recipes? In the outdoor markets of Italy and France, and recently in the United States, they are sold already cooked, to be taken home and added to a variety of dishes. This salad is a fine example of why beets should be eaten more often.

6   large beets, leaves and stems removed

Salt and freshly ground black pepper, to taste

¼   cup white wine vinegar

½   cup olive oil

1   teaspoon ground cumin

2   green onions, thinly sliced

Scrub the beets. Add 1 teaspoon salt to 2 to 3 quarts water in a saucepan and bring to a boil over high heat. Add the beets and bring back to a boil. Reduce heat and simmer, covered, until tender, about 1 hour. Drain and cool. Peel and julienne the beets. Toss the beets with salt and pepper.

Blend the vinegar and olive oil in a small bowl. Stir in the cumin and green onions and mix well. Pour the dressing over the beets, being careful not to crush them. Cover with plastic wrap and marinate for about 1 hour in the refrigerator before serving.

Serves 8   Pareve

moroccan carrot salad

When it comes to Moroccan salads, this one is my favorite. The combination of carrots (boiled, but still a little crunchy) tossed with cilantro, cumin, paprika, and ginger turns your taste buds on alert.

2   bay leaves

1   pound carrots, sliced ⅛ inch thick

1   cup white wine vinegar

1   cup oil

2   garlic cloves, chopped

1   tablespoon minced onion

1   tablespoon minced parsley

1   tablespoon minced cilantro

1   tablespoon ground cumin

1½   teaspoons paprika

¼   teaspoon ground ginger

1 tablespoon tomato paste

Salt and freshly ground black pepper, to taste

Bring 4 cups salted water and the bay leaves to a boil in a large saucepan over high heat. Add the carrots, return to a boil, then remove from heat. Drain the carrots, rinse them with cold water, and transfer to a serving dish.

Combine the vinegar, oil, garlic, onion, parsley, cilantro, cumin, paprika, ginger, and tomato paste in a food processor or blender and blend. Gently stir the mixture into the carrots. Season with salt and pepper and marinate in the refrigerator for 1 hour.

Serves 8   Pareve

lamb and vegetable couscous

Couscous, often referred to as Moroccan pasta, is steamed and served with steamed vegetables and lamb or chicken. Years ago this product required hours of work; today it is available in packages that read "ready in 5 minutes."

For Shabbat dinner, serve it Friday night and reheat at sundown Saturday. Michel serves a plain vegetable couscous at Koutoubia that is garnished with pine nuts, walnuts, and raisins.

2   tablespoons olive oil

6   lamb shanks, trimmed of fat

2   onions, diced

¼   cup chopped parsley

¼   cup chopped cilantro

8   saffron threads

Pinch of freshly grated nutmeg

Salt and freshly ground black pepper, to taste

3   large carrots, sliced

3   medium zucchini, sliced

2   cups diced butternut squash

3   medium turnips, diced

1½   cups instant couscous (about 12 ounces)

Heat the olive oil in a large pot over medium heat and brown the lamb shanks. Add half of the onions, 2 tablespoons each of the parsley and cilantro, 2 of the saffron threads, and the nutmeg, salt, and pepper. Add 2 cups water and bring to a boil. Reduce heat and simmer, covered, for 1½ hours, or until the meat falls away from the bone. Remove meat from the bones and discard bones. Keep warm.

Fill the bottom of a *couscoussière* (couscous steamer) or large pot with 2 cups water and the remaining saffron threads and bring to a boil. Add the remaining onion, the carrots, zucchini, butternut squash, and turnips and simmer, covered, until the vegetables are tender, about 20 minutes.

Steam the couscous in the top part of the couscoussière, or in a cheesecloth-lined colander that fits snugly above the simmering vegetables, until tender, about 5 minutes.

To serve, spoon the couscous onto a large serving platter, spreading it out to make a smooth, flat cake. Using a slotted spoon, arrange the vegetables and lamb around the edges of the couscous. Ladle the sauce from the lamb over the couscous and serve immediately.

Serves 6 to 8   Meat

chef's secrets

To ripen tomatoes, place them on a sunny windowsill. Don't refrigerate tomatoes.

If using long-cooking couscous, put it in a large bowl, cover with water (to wash out the starch), drain, and let dry for 20 minutes.

NEELA PANIZ
from chutney to chapatis

about the chef: It's difficult to believe that this chef rarely entered the kitchen when she was growing up in India. It was only after she moved to the United States and started to crave her native cuisine that she taught herself to cook. She worked on her recipes until she was satisfied they were perfect.

Urged by friends, Neela decided to open her own Los Angeles restaurant in 1985, and with partner David Chaparra, she created Bombay Café in West Los Angeles. Today this little restaurant garners big awards, and recently Bombay Café was declared the best Indian restaurant in the city by *Los Angeles* magazine. Food-lovers flock to the establishment, located in a minimall, to sample Neela's extraordinary curries, chutneys, and other delicacies. In a city filled with Indian restaurants and similar menus, Bombay Café stands out for its authentic dishes and purity of flavor. *The Bombay Cookbook*, a collection of Neela's recipes, has recently been published.

on judy's kitchen: Neela arrived on the set dressed in a colorful Indian sari, which she usually wears. Her black hair was pulled back and piled high on her head, exposing the traditional Indian marking on her forehead. She made quite a dramatic appearance on television, though with her very proper English accent she was professional, informative, and comfortable.

Neela arranged several Indian spices—including cardamom, cassia, cloves, coriander, and turmeric—on a large platter and talked about how best to use them. They were pre-measured for her chicken curry. With a flip of her wrist, she poured all the spices on top of onions sizzling in a pot. I wish the audience could have smelled the tantalizing aroma as the spices cooked with the onions.

Neela's food was magical, from the Green Apple–Coconut Chutney to the whole wheat Chapatis, which puffed up like balloons when transferred from the hot griddle to an open flame. Her knowledge of Indian breads is impressive, and she was very graceful as she demonstrated the traditional way to eat with your fingers, using bread as a scooper.

Neela's recipes make a terrific Rosh Hashanah or Yom Kippur break-the-fast meal, since they can be prepared in advance. Be sure to add a little honey—traditional for a sweet new year—to the chutney.

menu

~ Green Apple–Coconut Chutney

~ Sweet Tomato Chutney

~ Authentic Chicken Curry

~ Chapatis (Soft Whole Wheat Bread)

green apple–coconut chutney

Neela explained that no Indian curry is complete without a homemade fresh chutney. This is not a preserved chutney; it is made fresh daily from fruits, vegetables, and herbs at hand. This chutney has the crisp texture of chopped salad. But be warned: The garlic and chilies make it very spicy and pungent. It goes perfectly with Neela's chicken curry.

1   fresh coconut

8   to 10 Granny Smith apples, unpeeled, cored, and cut into eighths

1   cup cilantro, loosely packed

4   to 5 serrano chilies, stemmed but unseeded

1   tablespoon ground cumin

4   to 5 garlic cloves, to taste

Fresh lemon juice, to taste

Salt, to taste

Prepare the coconut as described on page 118.

Place the coconut chunks in a food processor and mince. Add the apples, cilantro, serranos, cumin, and garlic and process until finely chopped. Use a rubber spatula to scrape the mixture from the sides of the bowl. Add the lemon juice and salt to taste. Transfer to a large bowl. Cover with plastic wrap and refrigerate.

Makes 3 to 4 cups   Pareve

sweet tomato chutney

In most recipes, fresh tomatoes are preferred. For this chutney, canned tomatoes are perfectly acceptable; they make it much easier to prepare, without any loss of flavor. The jaggery adds a wonderful caramel-like taste. The vinegar contributes flavor and also helps preserve the chutney.

2   cans (16 ounces each) unsalted whole peeled tomatoes, drained

1   tablespoon corn or vegetable oil

1   tablespoon Panch Puran (see Note)

4   to 5 fresh kari leaves (see Note)

4   serrano chilies, sliced into ⅛-inch rounds

½   cup sugar, or to taste

¼   cup jaggery (see page 118)

2   tablespoons white vinegar

Coarsely chop the tomatoes in a food processor. Heat the oil in a nonaluminum saucepan over medium heat. Add the Panch Puran, kari leaves, and serranos. When the spattering stops, add the tomatoes, sugar, and jaggery. Reduce the heat and simmer until the jaggery melts.

Taste, and adjust sweetness if necessary. Cook over low heat for 20 minutes. Cool and stir in the vinegar.

Makes about 3 cups   Pareve

Note: Panch Puran is an Indian spice blend containing fennel, cumin, fenugreek, black mustard seeds, and nigella. It is available in Indian markets. Kari leaves are also available in Indian markets.

If you love curry, don't let the number of ingredients in this dish frighten you. It's really simple to prepare and well worth the effort. If you like it hotter, add more cayenne. Serve the curry with rice and one or both of Neela's chutneys.

This could be the Indian answer to the traditional Shabbat *cholent*, which is prepared before the Shabbat and kept warm for a Friday or Saturday meal.

1	piece (1½ inches) ginger, peeled
5	to 6 garlic cloves
2	serrano chilies
⅓	cup vegetable oil
2	small Spanish yellow onions, finely chopped

Hot water

2	black cardamom pods (see Note)
2	to 3 pieces cassia or cinnamon sticks
5	bay leaves
4	to 5 cloves
5	to 6 whole black peppercorns
2	tablespoons ground coriander
2	tablespoons ground cumin
¼	teaspoon turmeric
¼	teaspoon cayenne pepper
2	medium tomatoes, chopped
1	small chicken (1½ pounds), skin removed, and cut into 8 pieces
1½	teaspoons salt, or to taste
1	cup cilantro, chopped, for garnish

Mince the ginger, garlic, and serranos in a food processor and set aside.

Heat the oil in a large saucepan over medium-high heat. Add the onions and brown until they turn a deep red-brown, about 5 minutes. Add the ginger mixture and sauté for 1 minute. Add 1 to 2 tablespoons hot water to stop the browning of the onions and mix into a paste. Add the cardamom, cassia, bay leaves, cloves, peppercorns, coriander, cumin, turmeric, and cayenne. Add 1 or 2 tablespoons hot water. Brown for 2 to 3 minutes. Add the tomatoes and cook over high heat until the oil is separated from the paste, about 2 minutes. (May be prepared 1 or 2 days in advance and refrigerated until ready to use.)

Add the chicken and cook over medium heat until golden brown. Add the salt and ½ cup hot water. Cover and simmer for 30 minutes, or until the chicken is cooked through and almost falls off the bone when pierced with a fork.

To serve, garnish with cilantro.

Serves 4   Meat

Note: Black cardamom pods are available in Indian markets. They are an essential flavoring of the masala, or spice paste, used in this dish. If not available, substitute 2 teaspoons ground cardamom.

chapatis (soft whole wheat bread)

A chapati is the simplest Indian bread to make, and the most common. Indian whole wheat flour, called *ata*, is a soft flour that makes a delicate flat bread. Each chapati is browned on both sides on a special griddle called a *tava*. When placed over an open flame, the chapati puffs up like a balloon.

In India, people often do not use table utensils; they eat with their fingers. Since you can't pick up sauces with fingers, the bread acts as an edible utensil.

2½   cups ata (see Note)

¾   to 1 cup warm water

Place 2 cups of the flour in a large mixing bowl and form a well in the center. Slowly work in the water with your fingers, forming little crumbs. Continue working the dough with your fingers, adding water, until the dough is soft and pliable and no longer sticky. Knead well for 12 to 15 minutes, or until the dough comes away from your hands. Cover with a slightly damp kitchen towel and set aside for 5 to 10 minutes or use immediately.

Break the dough into pieces about 1 inch in diameter. Form each piece into a ball in the palm of your hands. Place the remaining ½ cup flour on a marble slab or wooden board and flatten each ball in the flour. Using a rolling pin, roll out into a 5 to 6-inch round, dredging in flour as needed.

Heat a tava, griddle, or cast-iron skillet and maintain a medium heat. Place 1 chapati on the tava and turn over once when small bubbles rise or blister. Turn over and brown the other side. Remove and cook over a gas stove-top burner until puffed up on 1 side. Serve immediately.

Makes about 10 to 12 chapatis   Pareve

Note: Ata is available in Indian markets. You may substitute whole wheat pastry flour.

chef's secrets

🌿 Before buying a coconut, shake it to make sure it's full of liquid. The fresher the coconut, the more liquid it will contain. Coconuts without liquid are likely to be spoiled. If the eyes of the coconut are not moldy, it is almost certainly fresh.

🌿 To prepare a coconut, puncture two of the three eyes by hammering them with the tip of an ice pick or screwdriver. Drain the coconut liquid into a measuring cup and reserve for other uses. Preheat the oven to 400°F. Bake the empty coconut for 15 minutes, then transfer to a chopping board. While hot, split the shell with a sharp blow of a hammer. The shell should fall away from the pieces of meat. If bits of meat still cling to the shell, cut them away with a small knife.

🌿 Jaggery is a type of raw sugar made from the juice of sugar cane or, occasionally, from the juice of certain palm trees. The juice is purified and boiled to produce sugar crystals lightly coated with molasses. Jaggery will keep indefinitely in a tightly covered jar. If jaggery is not available, make a substitute by combining 1 cup of dark brown sugar with 1 tablespoon of dark molasses.

🌿 Curry powder is a combination of spices, not a single spice. Neela combines many different spices to flavor her chicken, fish, or vegetable curries.

🌿 Other Indian breads include naan, which is cooked in a tandoor, and puffy puris, which are deep-fried. Parathas are similar to chapatis but are layered and cooked on a griddle.

TOMMY TANG
time for thai

about the chef: Thai food soared in popularity when Tommy Tang set foot in Los Angeles. The Bangkok native made eating this Southeast Asian cuisine fun when he opened his namesake restaurant in 1982. Hipper-than-thou Angelenos gave Tommy—and his chic menu—two enthusiastic thumbs up. Fans were charmed by his inventive dishes, which often combined Japanese, Indian, American, and European influences with traditional Thai. Complex seasonings and intense sauces became his trademark. Buoyed by his success, Tommy became one of the first Los Angeles chefs to go bicoastal when he opened a New York outpost. Then in 1994, he flung open the doors to Tommy Tang's in Pasadena's Old Town.

Tommy is all about high energy. His wife, Sandi, is an enthusiastic partner and assists him with the Tommy Tang products. Sandi is Jewish, and the Tangs celebrate all the Jewish holidays with their daughters, Aisha and Chyna. Sandi claims that Tommy makes the best potato latkes during Hanukkah for their friends.

If he isn't promoting his restaurants or cookbooks, Tommy is promoting his comprehensive line of spices and sauces under the Tommy Tang label. But he always finds time to be philanthropic; he often flies to Thailand to help raise money for local childrens' charities. Tommy's other favorite charities are the AIDS Project and helping the homeless. He remembers being homeless many times in his early life.

on judy's kitchen: Tommy's colorful clothing and engaging personality created a terrific television persona. Tommy bantered constantly and cooked effortlessly. He was also an expert teacher, imparting much useful information to the audience.

It was easy to adapt his Spicy Tuna Roll and signature Duck with Honey-Ginger Sauce for a kosher kitchen. Good thing it was easy, because it was a first for both Tommy and me. On camera I asked, "Tommy, have you ever cooked kosher?" He hesitated, grinned, and then said, "Kosher Thai cuisine? That's a first for me, Judy, so we can put it in the record book together."

Tommy and I worked so well together that we later demonstrated kosher Thai dishes at several Los Angeles food festivals. And since Tommy's guest appearance on *Judy's Kitchen*, he has his own Saturday morning national television series.

menu

~ Spicy Tuna Roll

~ Vegetarian Pad Thai

~ Tommy's Duck with Honey-Ginger Sauce

spicy tuna roll

This easy-to-make version of what a master sushi chef prepares in a Japanese restaurant tastes just as good as the real thing.

8	ounces sushi grade ahi tuna, ground
2	tablespoons Tommy's Mayonnaise (recipe follows)
2	tablespoons finely sliced green onions
1	tablespoon Tommy Tang's Thai Seasoning (see Note)
1	tablespoon sesame oil
1	tablespoon sesame seeds
2	cups cooked Sushi Rice (recipe follows)
2	sheets nori, halved (see Note)
1	tablespoon wasabi powder mixed with 1 tablespoon warm water or fresh horseradish (see Note)
6	ounces pickled ginger, for garnish (see Note)

Soy sauce, for dipping

Combine the tuna, mayonnaise, green onions, Thai seasoning, sesame oil, and sesame seeds in a medium bowl and mix well. Spread an equal amount of rice smoothly over each nori sheet. Smear the rice with wasabi, lengthwise down the center. Wet your hands with water and divide the tuna mixture into four parts. Place a portion on top of the rice, lengthwise down the center. Working with 1 roll at a time, hold the nori with both hands and roll up slowly until ends meet. Drape a piece of plastic wrap over the roll and top with a bamboo sushi mat. Squeeze gently until the roll is firm and holds together. Remove the plastic and the bamboo mat. Repeat the process to make 3 more rolls.

Dip a sharp knife into cold water and let the excess water drip off. Cut each roll crosswise into 6 slices. Arrange the rolls, cut side up, on plates and garnish with pickled ginger. Serve with soy sauce.

Makes 4 rolls; serves 6   Pareve

Notes: Thai seasoning is a combination of garlic, black pepper, white pepper, chili powder, and cayenne.

Nori is dark green sheets of dried Japanese seaweed, used for wrapping sushi.

Wasabi is powdered green Japanese horseradish, used to give a pungency to sushi. Use sparingly; it's extremely hot.

Pickled ginger is a hot sweet-tart condiment that is served with sushi to refresh the palate between courses.

Thai seasoning, nori, wasabi, and pickled ginger can be found in most supermarkets in the Japanese section.

sushi rice

Sushi rice is a combination of boiled rice and a sweet vinegar rice stock. It's easy to prepare at home.

Sushi Rice Stock:

1½	cups rice vinegar
¼	cup sake or dry white wine
2	tablespoons sugar
½	tablespoon sugar
4	cups hot water
1	cup Japanese short-grain rice, rinsed in cold water

To make the Sushi Rice Stock, combine the rice vinegar, 1 cup water, sake, sugar, and salt in a medium nonaluminum saucepan over high heat and bring to a boil. Reduce the heat to low and simmer for 15 minutes. Cool. Measure out 2 tablespoons and reserve rest for later use. (Stock can be kept in the refrigerator for 4 weeks; freeze for longer storage.)

Combine the water and rice in a medium saucepan over high heat and bring to a boil. Reduce the heat to medium and cook until the rice grains are swollen, about 15 minutes. Transfer the rice to a strainer and drain well. Transfer to a large bowl, add the 2 tablespoons stock, and mix well with a spatula. Cool to lukewarm, then use for preparing sushi.

Makes about 4 cups   Pareve

tommy's mayonnaise

1   egg white

1   tablespoon rice vinegar

¼   teaspoon white pepper

2   tablespoons olive oil

Combine the egg white, vinegar, and pepper in a small bowl and whisk to blend. Slowly drizzle in the olive oil, whisking constantly until the mixture is firm.

Makes about ½ cup   Pareve

vegetarian pad thai

This spicy noodle dish can stand alone as a main course for lunch. For dinner, serve it as a first course, followed by Tommy's Duck with Honey-Ginger Sauce.

¾   pound pad thai noodles (see Note) or egg noodles

¼   cup olive oil

2   ounces firm brown tofu, diced (see Note)

1   egg

3   tablespoons tamarind juice (see Note)

1   tablespoon rice vinegar

1   tablespoon sugar or honey

2   tablespoons Vegetable Stock (page 166)

2   teaspoons paprika

½   teaspoon crushed red pepper or cayenne pepper

¾   cup sliced onions

½   cup diced celery

3   tablespoons crushed unsalted peanuts, toasted

3   ounces fresh bean sprouts

2   tablespoons thinly sliced leeks, for garnish

Soak the noodles in 8 cups cold water in a large bowl for 45 minutes. Drain in a colander and set aside.

Heat the olive oil in a large nonstick skillet, over high heat. Add the tofu and sauté until lightly browned, about 1 minute. Stir in the egg and tamarind juice. Add the rice vinegar, sugar, stock, paprika, red pepper, onions, and celery and stir-fry for 1 minute. Add the drained noodles and peanuts and cook, stirring constantly, until heated through and well mixed, about 2 minutes. Toss in the bean sprouts.

To serve, transfer to a large platter and sprinkle with leeks.

Serves 6   Pareve.

Note: Pad thai noodles, brown tofu, and tamarind juice, are available in Asian markets.

tommy's duck with honey-ginger sauce

Kosher ducks are usually only available frozen, so most people who keep kosher don't prepare them very often. This recipe is so simple, yet so flavorful, that it's well worth working with frozen duck. Be sure frozen duck is well packaged; thaw it completely in the refrigerator before using, about one to one and a half days.

½   cup diced onions

¼   cup peeled and diced fresh ginger

½   cup light soy sauce

2   kosher ducklings (5½ to 6 pounds each), halved, skin on

Honey-Ginger Sauce (recipe follows)

3   cups vegetable oil, for frying

Finely chop the onions and ginger in a food processor. Add the soy sauce and 1 cup water and blend. Thoroughly coat the ducks with the mixture, cover with plastic wrap, and refrigerate for at least 6 hours or overnight.

Preheat the oven to 350°F.

Remove the ducks from the marinade, wiping off the excess and reserving the marinade. Place the ducks in a roasting pan and strain the marinade over them. Bake for 1½ hours, or until the duck is tender, basting every 15 minutes with the juices in the pan.

While the duck is roasting, prepare the honey-ginger sauce and keep warm.

Heat the oil in a large nonstick saucepan or deep-fryer to 350°F. Place 1 duck half, skin side down, in the oil and fry until the skin is crisp, 3 to 5 minutes. Remove the duck with tongs and drain on paper towels. Repeat the process with the remaining duck halves, frying them one at a time.

To serve, cut off the legs and wings from the duck; slice the breast, and trim off as much fat as possible. Arrange breast slices on plates along with a duck leg. Pour the honey-ginger sauce over the duck and serve at once.

Serves 4 to 6   Meat

honey-ginger sauce

1   cup honey

¼   cup plum sauce (see Note) or grape jelly

¼   cup soy sauce

¼   cup peeled and sliced fresh ginger

1   teaspoon flour mixed with 2 tablespoons cold water

Combine ½ cup water, honey, plum sauce, soy sauce, and ginger in a heavy saucepan over high heat and bring to a boil. Whisk in the flour-water mixture, reduce heat to low, and simmer until the sauce is syrupy, about 20 minutes. Keep warm.

Makes about 1½ cups   Pareve

Note: Plum sauce is a sweet-and-sour sauce that is common in Chinese cooking. It is available in most supermarkets and Asian markets.

YUJEAN KANG

one-man chinese revolution

about the chef: If any American-based chef has revolutionized Chinese cuisine, it's Yujean Kang. Walk into his namesake restaurants in Pasadena and West Hollywood and be prepared to enter a new world of gastronomy. Yujean's refined cooking style showcases traditional Chinese fare with contemporary flair. Rather than zooming in on one region, this chef often incorporates elements from many. And he's never afraid to put a Western spin on a dish—perhaps through an ingredient, often with a technique.

The roots of Yujean's culinary career hark back to his homeland of Taiwan. His parents were the cook-owners of a restaurant in Taipei, and Yujean worked in the family business in many capacities, from busboy to apprentice chef. When Yujean was a teenager, the Kangs moved to the United States. Yujean then secured jobs in a variety of Chinese restaurants learning the American style of restaurant operations.

At the young age of twenty-three, Yujean and his family opened Yujean's Modern Cuisine of China in Albany, a small community in Northern California. As executive chef of this cutting-edge restaurant, Yujean received major kudos. For instance, *Wine Spectator* magazine showcased the establishment in an article titled "Eight Best Meals of the Year." Encouraged by his success, Yujean and his wife, Yvonne, moved to Southern California to open the first Yujean Kang's in Pasadena. Again, the chef was greeted with acclaim—much of it national. In 1996, the couple opened their second restaurant in West Hollywood. The new eatery is receiving as much attention as the Pasadena flagship and is creating an even wider audience of admirers for Yujean.

on judy's kitchen: Yujean Kang was another first-timer to the television world. Although soft-spoken and a bit shy, he needed few words to explain his cooking style. His techniques were awesome; watching him slice, dice, chop, and stir-fry, I realized that the audience was about to be as dazzled as I was.

Yujean had agreed to demonstrate his Picture in the Snow. This soup is a showstopper. An intensely flavored chicken broth is topped with a "canvas" made from egg whites whipped to a meringue and steamed. Vegetables cut into various shapes create the portrait. Following Yujean's design is surprisingly simple, but you should feel free to create one of your own.

menu

~ Picture in the Snow

~ Chinese Eggplant with Garlic and Cilantro

~ Chicken with Pungent Garlic

The most beautiful garnish imaginable—chicken soup meets oriental magic! A deeply flavored homemade chicken soup forms a rich background to this unique dish. In a more picturesque rendition of the classic Cantonese West Lake Soup, Yujean composes a picture with cut-out carrot, red bell pepper, and parsley flowers on a snowy canvas of meringue that floats on the soup.

4   cups Chicken Stock (page 167)

3   tablespoons soy sauce

1   tablespoon sugar

Pinch of salt

Pinch of white pepper

2   teaspoons dry white wine

1   tablespoon vinegar

Few drops of sesame oil

2   teaspoons cornstarch

4   shiitake mushrooms, stems removed, caps julienned

6   enoki mushrooms

3   or 4 large leaves napa cabbage, julienned

2   cooked chicken breasts, julienned

Garnish for the Meringue Picture (recipe follows)

Combine the stock, soy sauce, sugar, salt, pepper, wine, vinegar, sesame oil, and cornstarch in a large saucepan over high heat. Bring to a boil, add the mushrooms and cabbage, reduce heat, and simmer for 10 minutes. Just before serving, stir in the chicken breast.

While the soup is cooking, prepare the meringue picture.

To serve, reheat the soup and ladle it into soup bowls. Place a plate with meringue in a steamer, cover, and steam for about 3 seconds. Carefully slide the meringue into a bowl of soup, allowing it to float on top. Repeat with the remaining bowls of soup and meringues. Serve immediately.

Serves 4   Meat

2   tablespoons vegetable oil

4   egg whites, kept separate

4   diamond-shape slices of carrot

¼   cup dried Chinese black mushrooms, soaked, drained, and julienned (optional)

4   chives

Red bell pepper strips

Cilantro sprigs and stems

Grease the surface of four 5-inch round plates with vegetable oil. Beat 1 egg white until fluffy but not stiff. Spread over the greased plate and smooth the meringue with a knife or a spatula. Arrange the vegetables in a design on top of the meringue to create a picture. Repeat the process with the remaining plates and refrigerate.

Makes 4 meringue pictures   Pareve

chinese eggplant with garlic and cilantro

Of all the hot-and-spicy Chinese dishes, this is my favorite. Instead of julienning Japanese eggplants, Yujean cuts them on the diagonal into thick shapes. This vegetable dish can accompany chicken or fish. It is also substantial enough for a main course when served with a bowl of rice.

For ease of preparation, measure all the ingredients for the sauce in advance.

2   Japanese eggplants

½   cup cornstarch

2   cups peanut or safflower oil, for frying

3   to 4 garlic cloves, minced

½   to 1 tablespoon chili paste

1   tablespoon peeled and minced fresh ginger

1   tablespoon rice wine

1   tablespoon soy sauce

Pinch of sugar

1   tablespoon rice vinegar

1   teaspoon sesame oil

9   sprigs cilantro

1   tablespoon cornstarch dissolved in ¼ cup water

1   tablespoon sliced chives, for garnish

Slice the eggplant at an angle into 1½-inch-thick shapes. Toss the sliced eggplant in the cornstarch and shake off the excess.

Heat the oil in a large wok to a high temperature and quickly deep-fry the eggplant, tossing constantly, for about 3 minutes, or until brown. Transfer the eggplant to a strainer set over a pot and allow the oil to drain off. Drain the wok, reserving the oil.

Reheat the wok, add 2 tablespoons of the oil, and stir-fry the garlic, chili paste, ginger, rice wine, soy sauce, sugar, rice vinegar, and sesame oil for a few seconds to release the flavor. Add the drained eggplant, cilantro, and dissolved cornstarch. Bring to a boil, stirring, until the sauce thickens slightly. Remove from heat.

To serve, spoon the eggplant into a serving plate and garnish with the chives.

Serves 4   Pareve

chicken with pungent garlic

Marinating is the secret to this chicken's tenderness and unforgettable flavor. Serve it with bowls of rice.

2   cups vegetable or safflower oil, for frying

3   garlic cloves, thinly sliced

1   tablespoon dry white wine

1   cup Chicken Stock (page 167)

1   egg white

1   tablespoon cornstarch

Pinch of salt

Pinch of white pepper

1   pound chicken breast, boned, skinned, and julienned

4   to 6 baby corn

1   medium zucchini, sliced

Garlic Sauce (see below)

1   teaspoon chili paste

1   teaspoon minced garlic

1   teaspoon peeled and chopped fresh ginger

2   tablespoons dry white wine

2   tablespoons soy sauce

Pinch of sugar

2   tablespoons rice vinegar

½   tablespoon sesame oil

1   teaspoon cornstarch

Heat the oil in a wok to a high temperature and deep-fry the garlic until crisp. Remove the garlic with a slotted spoon and set aside.

Combine the wine, stock, egg white, cornstarch, salt, pepper, and 2 tablespoons of the oil in a medium bowl. Add the chicken and marinate for 15 minutes.

Reheat the oil in the wok to a low temperature and add the marinated chicken breasts, baby corn, and zucchini. Cook slowly until barely cooked. Transfer the chicken mixture to a strainer set over a pot to drain off the excess oil.

To make the Garlic Sauce, heat a clean wok and sauté the chili paste, garlic, and ginger. Add the wine, soy sauce, sugar, vinegar, and sesame oil. Mix in the cornstarch and simmer until golden and bubbly. Add the drained chicken mixture and toss to coat. Sprinkle with the crisp garlic and toss.

To serve, spoon the chicken mixture into a heated serving bowl.

Serves 4   Meat

chef's secrets

❦ Coat food with cornstarch when frying to protect it from absorbing too much oil.

❦ For easier frying, place a stainless steel strainer over a pot and fill the pot with 2 cups of oil. Place near the stove. Use a ladle to add oil to the wok and transfer the fried food to the strainer to allow the excess oil to drain off.

❦ To season a wok, pour in 1 cup of oil, swirl to coat the wok, and heat the oil. Then pour the oil into a large pot. Add the required amount of oil to the wok and reheat.

JONATHAN WAXMAN

coast-to-coast cook

about the chef: Jonathan Waxman is one Californian who took New York by storm. When he opened Jams restaurant in Manhattan in 1984, the buzz became a roar. He was one of the first to introduce California cuisine to the Big Apple, and New Yorkers responded by turning out in droves to eat his wood-fired grilled chicken and crisp french fries.

A native Californian, Jonathan was initiated into the world of haute cuisine in 1976 at France's famed La Varenne cooking school. He returned to the West Coast to work for Alice Waters—an innovator of California cooking—at Chez Panisse in Berkeley. With such top-drawer classic and contemporary training, small wonder that Jonathan was so well received when he took over as chef of Michael's restaurant in Santa Monica.

With the success of Jams, Jonathan remained in New York to open two other restaurants, Bud's and Hulot's. He even ventured to London and cloned Jams there. Then, tired of working at the stove, he left New York and consulted for several years at restaurants around the country. He moved back to New York to work with Ark Restaurants, a company running some thirty dining establishments nationwide. Jonathan devised many menus, focusing on simple, seasonal fare with broad appeal. Currently, he is consulting and writing.

on judy's kitchen: Jonathan arrived on the set looking like a Californian. His curly hair cascaded loosely down to his shoulders. Our director, Harvey Lehr, had to coax Jonathon to pull his thick locks back into a ponytail. He felt very at ease on-camera, and his relaxed manner really came across. He was completely focused on our cooking together. He gave clear instructions and was quick to respond to my questions.

Jonathan developed his Chicken Poached in Spicy Court Bouillon just for the show. It's a take-off on the French pot-au-feu, and it tastes wonderful. Jonathan describes his food as "earthbound"; it isn't time-consuming or precious.

For his endive salad, he used tangerines from my backyard tree and tossed the fruit with beets and pecans. The salad was colorful—absolutely striking—and it didn't require a lot of work. Clever but not fussy, that's Jonathan's style.

menu

~ Endive Salad with Tangerine Sections,
   Beets, and Olives
~ Chicken Poached in a Spicy Court Bouillon with
   Aromatic Vegetables and Mustard Sauce

endive salad with tangerine sections, beets, and olives

This colorful salad, combining nuts, fruit, and vegetables, is typical of this chef's ingenuity.

1½ cups pecan halves

Salt, to taste

3 small yellow beets, with tops

3 small red beets, with tops

5 seedless tangerines or 4 oranges, seeded

⅔ cup olive oil

1 cup small niçoise or Italian black olives, pitted

4 heads of belgian endive

6 sprigs cilantro or chervil, for garnish

Preheat the oven to 450°F. Line a baking sheet with foil.

Place the pecans on the baking sheet, sprinkle lightly with salt, and toast until brown, about 4 minutes. Do not overtoast or they can turn bitter. Let cool.

Remove the leaves from the beets, discarding any tough ones but keeping the rest for salads or cooked greens. Wash and dry the beets and place yellow and red beets in separate saucepans with cold salted water. Bring to a boil, reduce heat, and simmer until tender, 45 minutes to 1 hour. Skin will peel off easily. Cut into small wedges and keep separate.

Squeeze juice from 1 tangerine and set aside. You should have ½ cup juice. Peel and section the remaining tangerines.

Combine the pecans, tangerine juice, and olive oil in a large bowl. Add the olives and tangerine sections. Add the beets and toss gently.

Cut 1 inch from the bottom of each head of Belgian endive and discard. Cut 2 heads crosswise into thin slices. Separate the other 2 heads into individual leaves.

To serve, arrange the endive leaves in a circular pattern on a large platter or individual salad plates. Carefully arrange the beet mixture in the center of the endive leaves, reserving the juices. Add the julienned endives to the bowl with the reserved juices and toss to coat. Arrange on top of the salad. Garnish with sprigs of cilantro or chervil.

Serves 8   Pareve

chicken poached in a spicy court bouillon with aromatic vegetables and mustard sauce

At New York's Jams restaurant, Jonathan was renowned for his oversized plate of grilled free-range chicken with aromatic vegetables. This updated version is virtually fat free since the chicken and vegetables are poached. A mustard sauce gives the broth some zip, much like a rouille does for bouillabaisse. Don't be alarmed by the list of ingredients—this is an easy dish to prepare.

1 roasting chicken (4 to 5 pounds)

2 onions

1 head garlic, cloves separated

3 shallots

6 *each* small red and white new potatoes, scrubbed and halved lengthwise

4 shiitake mushrooms, stemmed

4 small turnips, quartered

2 small parsnips, halved

4 small carrots, scrubbed and halved

2   stalks fennel or celery, quartered

8   radishes, scrubbed

1   large leek, halved and soaked in cold water

2   bay leaves

10 to 15 whole black peppercorns

1   anaheim chili, roasted, peeled, and seeded

1   jalapeño chili, roasted, peeled, and seeded

½   teaspoon salt

10 sprigs parsley, washed and tied in a bundle

6   sprigs tarragon, washed and tied in a bundle

Mustard Sauce (recipe follows)

1 baguette, thinly sliced and toasted

Preheat the oven to 450°F.

Truss the chicken and set aside.

Peel the onions, cut in half, and place in a baking dish, cut side down. Bake for 30 minutes, or until golden brown.

Combine the garlic, shallots, potatoes, mushrooms, turnips, parsnips, carrots, fennel, radishes, and leek in a large bowl.

Pour enough cold water to poach the chicken and vegetables into a large pot. Add the roasted onions, bay leaves, and peppercorns. Bring to a boil, reduce the heat, and simmer for 30 minutes. Add the chilies. Add the chicken, vegetables, parsley, and tarragon to the pot and simmer for 30 minutes. Add the salt and continue to cooking for 30 minutes, or until the chicken is tender. Using a slotted spoon, remove the chicken and vegetables and keep warm in 2 cups of the broth. Strain the remaining broth and boil for 15 minutes.

While the chicken is cooking, prepare the mustard sauce.

To serve, remove the string from the chicken, separate into 8 portions, and place in the center of a large platter. Arrange the vegetables around the chicken. Ladle the broth into large shallow soup bowls and float 2 or 3 toasted bread slices on top. Place a tablespoonful of mustard sauce in the broth. Serve the broth as a side dish and pass the platter of chicken and vegetables at the table.

Serves 8   Meat

mustard sauce

1   red bell pepper, roasted, peeled, and seeded (see page 165)

1   heaping tablespoon whole-grain mustard

4   garlic cloves from broth, peeled

½   cup broth from pot

1   teaspoon salt

1   teaspoon black peppercorns

Place the bell pepper, mustard, garlic, and broth in a food processor or blender. Process until smooth. Transfer to a bowl. Add salt and pepper.

Makes about ¾ cup   Meat

chef's secrets

❧ Use vinegar instead of lemon juice to remove beet stains from your hands.

❧ When peeling raw beets or working with cooked beets, place a dish towel on the work surface to avoid staining the counter.

BRUCE AIDELLS
the sausage king

about the chef: Bruce Aidells has quite the scholarly background for a chef. Born and raised in California, he graduated from the University of California at Berkeley and received a Ph.D. from the University of California at Santa Cruz. While doing research in London, Bruce began to experiment with sausage recipes in his spare time. He worked on improving British bangers and experimented with chorizo and Italian and Provençal sausages.

Returning to Berkeley, Bruce became a chef at the popular Poulet restaurant, where he continued perfecting his sausage making. He was soon recognized as one of the chefs who made Berkeley a byword for innovative cuisine—and as the Bay Area's premier sausage-maker. In 1983, he founded Aidells Sausage Company and soon his hand-crafted charcuterie was a menu staple at leading restaurants nationwide.

Says Bruce: "The sausage phenomenon took on a life of its own. I began making and selling a wide range of sausages—andouille, duck, Italian, and kielbasa—to restaurants around the country. The enthusiastic response from chefs, butchers, retailers, and home cooks testifies to the interest in sausages in America today."

Bruce's published work includes numerous magazine articles, two books in the California Culinary Academy series, and an *American Sausage* cookbook. He is also the author or co-author with Denis Kelly of six other books, including *Hot Links and Country Flavors*, and *Real Beer and Good Eats*.

on judy's kitchen: Bruce arrived on the set wearing a beige chef's jacket—he got the color by soaking his whites in tea—and a brown leather cap. He was full of good humor and lots of energy, eager to impart his enthusiasm for sausage making. Bruce shared recipes from his sausage company and his sausage cookbook, comparing them to the traditional knockwurst served in most Jewish delis.

Bruce explained that sausages are wonderful flavoring agents for soups, stews, salads, pâtés, and other hearty dishes. Surprisingly, the whole process of sausage making was much easier than I had expected. Although Americans love sausages, we seldom think of making them. But good kosher sausages are hard to come by, so here's an opportunity to prepare your own for family and friends. Homemade kosher sausage was almost unheard of—that is, until Bruce perfected the process. No wonder he is called "The Sausage King."

menu

~ Wilted Cabbage and Roasted Walnut Salad

~ Turkey Sausage with Fruit Liqueur

~ Romanian Kosher Beef Sausage

wilted cabbage and roasted walnut salad

A combination of crunchy walnuts and zesty slaw is an appealing base for savory sausages. Serve this salad warm with the beef sausage, or at room temperature with the turkey sausage.

4   tablespoons (½ stick) unsalted margarine

½   head of cabbage, cored and shredded

¼   teaspoon salt

½   teaspoon freshly ground black pepper

3   tablespoons cider vinegar

1   tablespoon soy sauce

½   cup walnuts, toasted (see page 165)

Melt the margarine in a large sauté pan, over medium heat. Add the cabbage, salt, and pepper and toss, coating with the margarine. Cover and cook for 7 minutes, stirring occasionally, until the cabbage is wilted but still crisp. Pour in the vinegar and soy sauce and cook for 2 minutes, uncovered. Serve warm, right from the pan. Garnish with roasted walnuts.

Serves 4   Pareve

turkey sausage with fruit liqueur

Ground turkey contains very little fat, so be careful not to overcook the sausages or they will be tough. Also, turkey meat tends to be bland, so it needs lots of spices. The fennel seeds add a pungent flavor.

2¼   pounds boned turkey thigh meat including fat on thigh, cut into pieces

½   teaspoon ground sage

1   teaspoon dried thyme

1   teaspoon fennel seeds

1   teaspoon sweet Hungarian paprika

⅛   teaspoon ground allspice

1   teaspoon minced garlic

2   teaspoons coarsely ground black pepper

1   tablespoon kosher salt

¼   cup orange flavored liqueur, such as Grand Marnier

2   teaspoons honey

Grind the turkey meat and fat through a ¼-inch plate. Transfer to a large bowl and add the sage, thyme, fennel seeds, paprika, allspice, garlic, pepper, salt, fruit liqueur, honey, and 2 to 3 tablespoons water. Using your hands, squeeze the mixture, working in spices at the same time, until thoroughly combined. Do not overwork. Shape the mixture into patties or logs and wrap in plastic wrap as described on page 135. (Store in the refrigerator for up to 3 days or in the freezer for 2 months.)

Makes twelve 5-inch sausages   Meat

romanian kosher beef sausage

This is Bruce's version of the beef sausages served at the famous Sammy's Romanian Kosher Restaurant in New York. These garlicky sausages make a great sandwich with mustard and sauerkraut. Serve with the cabbage salad on the side. I like to serve them for our family picnics with lots of dill pickles.

3   pounds lean beef

1¼   ounces fatty beef, such as short ribs

4   ounces firm beef fat

5   teaspoons kosher salt

1   tablespoon coarsely ground black pepper

2   teaspoons ground coriander

Pinch ground allspice

1   bay leaf, crushed

Pinch ground cloves

1   teaspoon dry mustard

2   tablespoons whole yellow mustard seeds

2   tablespoons minced garlic

2   teaspoons sugar

1   teaspoon saltpeter (see Note)

Plastic wrap or lamb or beef casings

Grind the lean beef through the ⅜-inch plate of a meat grinder. Grind the fatty beef and fat through the ¼-inch plate. Combine the ground meats, salt, pepper, coriander, allspice, bay leaves, cloves, dry mustard and mustard seeds, garlic, sugar, and saltpeter in a large bowl. Squeeze the meat mixture with your hands, working in the spices at the same time. Do not overwork. Add just enough water to be able to work in the spices and knead until well blended.

If using plastic wrap, lay about 3 feet of it flat on the work area. Shape the meat mixture into a sausage form and place on the plastic wrap about 3 inches from the long edge. Leave a 4-inch margin on both ends. Take the plastic wrap closest to you and cover the sausage neatly, rolling tightly into a long sausage shape. Pull tightly on both ends while twisting like candy wrap. Tie each end with string, leaving about

1½ inches of space between the sausage and the string for air space. Pinch at 5-inch intervals, tying each with a string to create 6 links. Repeat with the remaining meat mixture. (If using casings, see page 167.) Refrigerate sausage immediately and cook within 2 days.

To cook, drop sausages into simmering water and poach 10 to 15 minutes, turning halfway during poaching. Do not boil. Plunge into cold water to cool. Remove the plastic wrap and strings. Sauté in a lightly oiled skillet until golden brown, stirring occasionally.

To broil, poach, then remove the plastic wrap and strings. Place sausages on a foil-lined broiler pan and broil 3 inches from the heat, turning frequently to brown evenly. Or grill on a rack over hot coals, turning frequently to brown evenly.

Makes about 12 sausages   Meat

Note: Saltpeter (potassium nitrate) gives the characteristic red color to many sausages and also acts as a preservative. If you are concerned about consuming nitrates, bicarbonate of soda may be substituted, but it is not as effective.

chef's secrets

❧ Fresh sausages can be made from raw, ground, or chopped meat; fish or vegetable mixtures. They should be highly seasoned. The mixture can be stuffed into casings, if kosher casings are available (Bruce uses the more delicate sheep intestines), or shaped into patties, loaves, or logs and rolled in plastic wrap. Patties or logs can be poached, fried, grilled, or baked.

❧ The meat should be very cold, but do not use frozen meat. Be sure to use the freshest meat available.

CHRIS SCHLESINGER
thrill of the grill

a b o u t   t h e   c h e f : Bold food, bold flavors—that's Chris Schlesinger's style. This spirited chef is drawn to spices and peppers as if they were magnets. He's also an aficionado of grilling. He'll toss almost anything onto the grill and transform it into an irresistible meal. Chris first discovered his love of grilled food as a child in Virginia. His father used to barbecue steaks until they turned crusty and black outside but were close to raw inside.

Chris left college to work in restaurants. He started as a dishwasher and worked his way up to line cook. Then he decided to get serious and enrolled in the Culinary Institute of America at Hyde Park, New York. After graduating in 1977, Chris found jobs in a whopping thirty-five restaurants. He traveled extensively, and several times entered the International Barbecue Contest in Memphis, Tennessee, where he won many awards.

In 1986, he and partner Cary Wheaton opened Boston's East Coast Grill. In 1989, they debuted Jake & Earl's Dixie Barbecue next door. *People* magazine deemed their barbecue palace America's best. In 1996, Chris won the prestigious James Beard Perrier-Jouët Award for Best Chef of the Northeast. Chris's credits roll on. He's co-author (with John Willoughby) of several books, including *The Thrill of the Grill*, which won one of the coveted James Beard cookbook awards. He also penned a new book with Willoughby, entitled *Lettuce in Your Kitchen,* and the about-to-be-released *License to Grill.*

o n   j u d y ' s   k i t c h e n : Chris trekked in from Boston to appear on the show. We had never met before he arrived on the set, but he greeted me like an old friend. He chose not to wear a chef's jacket, finding it somewhat contrived for television.

Chris was so personable and relaxed, it was easy to converse and cook together. In fact, we almost forgot about the cameras and allowed ourselves to have a good time. I'll never forget the aromas swirling around the set. His use of fragrant herbs and spices made everyone's mouth water. We couldn't wait to sample his specialties.

menu

~ José's Jícama Slaw

~ Avocado Stuffed with Seared Tuna

~ Grilled Steak, Cuban Style

josé's jícama slaw

Coleslaw is an all-American favorite. Most recipes combine cabbage and carrots. But when you add jícama and cilantro, the slaw gains a south-of-the-border dimension. One of Chris's talented chefs, José Velasquz, created this salad. Chris and I agreed that red or green bell peppers would contribute a splash of needed color.

5   cups grated green cabbage

2   cups grated carrots

2   cups peeled and julienned jícama

Cilantro Dressing (recipe follows)

Combine the cabbage, carrots, and jícama in a large bowl. Pour the dressing over the vegetables and toss until combined.

Serves 8 to 10   Pareve

cilantro dressing

1   cup chopped cilantro

½   cup yellow mustard

½   cup ketchup

¼   cup white vinegar

2   teaspoons sugar

1   garlic clove, minced

Salt and freshly ground black pepper, to taste

Blend the cilantro, mustard, ketchup, vinegar, sugar, and garlic in a food processor or blender until smooth. Season with salt and pepper. Cover with plastic wrap and refrigerate until ready to use.

Makes about 3 cups   Pareve

avocado stuffed with seared tuna

The key to this appealing salad is to grill the tuna over high heat until it's seared—dark on the outside but still a bit raw on the inside. The lime juice continues to "cook" the tuna for two hours after it's grilled, like a seviche.

1   pound tuna steak, 2 inches thick

Salt and freshly ground black pepper, to taste

Juice of 4 limes

1   tomato, coarsely chopped

1   medium red onion, diced

1   red bell pepper, seeded and finely chopped

2   tablespoons chopped cilantro

2   tablespoons olive oil

2   ripe avocados, halved, pitted, and peeled

½   medium head green cabbage, thinly sliced

3   radishes, finely sliced, for garnish

1   lime, cut into rounds, for garnish

cilantro sprigs, for garnish

Prepare the grill and heat until extra hot.

Sprinkle the tuna generously with salt and pepper. Grill the tuna quickly until well browned on both sides, 2 to 3 minutes per side. Let cool, then cut into ¼-inch slices. Place sliced tuna in a shallow pan, cover with lime juice, and marinate for 2 to 3 hours, covered, in the refrigerator.

Transfer the tuna to a large bowl and sprinkle with the tomato, onion, bell pepper, cilantro, and olive oil, reserving some of the mixture for garnish. Season with salt and pepper and toss lightly.

To serve, place each avocado half, cut side up, on a bed of sliced cabbage on a large platter or individual plates. Put 2 to 3 slices of the tuna on each avocado half, and spoon the remaining tomato-pepper mixture on top. Garnish with radishes, lime, and cilantro sprigs.

Serves 4   Pareve

grilled steak, cuban style

This grilled rib-eye steak salad typifies Chris's style. Tabasco, cumin, chili powder, and cilantro really enliven the dish. The steak develops a wonderful crusty exterior since it's seasoned and cooked at a very high temperature. Serve it with rice and beans.

2½   pounds rib-eye steak, about 1½ inches thick

Kosher salt and coarsely cracked black pepper, to taste

1   large red onion, diced

1   red bell pepper, seeded and diced

1   green bell pepper, seeded and diced

10   radishes, sliced very thin

¼   cup olive oil

1   tablespoon Tabasco sauce

1   tablespoon minced garlic

2   tablespoons finely chopped parsley

2   tablespoons finely chopped cilantro

1   tablespoon ground cumin

1   tablespoon chili powder

6   tablespoons lime juice (about 3 limes)

Prepare the grill and heat until very hot.

Generously season the meat with salt and pepper and grill until dark brown and very crusty on the outside and pink inside, 4 to 6 minutes per side. Let stand for about 5 minutes to cool. Cut the meat into ½-inch cubes and place in a large bowl. Add the red onion, bell peppers, and radishes and mix well. Add the olive oil, Tabasco, garlic, parsley, cilantro, cumin, and chili powder and toss well to coat the meat.

Just before serving, blend in the lime juice.

Serves 4   Meat

chef's secrets

❧ Store avocados in a plastic container or a brown paper bag, away from sunlight, to ripen.

❧ Jicama is a crisp, sweet root vegetable that looks like a large tan turnip. When peeled and sliced, though, it is white and tastes more like an apple or potato. In Mexico, slices of jicama are served with a sprinkling of chili powder.

❧ Kosher salt tastes less salty than table salt and dissolves smoothly and quickly in hot liquid.

BRUCE MARDER
modern tex-mex cuisine

about the chef: When you dine in a Bruce Marder restaurant, it's difficult to believe this chef was once more interested in cavities than cuisine. Bruce was planning to become a dentist, but decided to take a year off from his studies to travel. In Morocco, he met some European chefs who convinced him that cooking might be his true passion. "It was fate," declares Bruce.

Bruce first created gastronomic shock waves at West Beach Café, his Santa Monica restaurant. This establishment was one of the first to serve what's now recognized as California cuisine. Bruce later opened Rebecca's, specializing in Mexican cuisine, close by and was greeted with much enthusiasm by the dining public. This energetic chef also designed and was the consulting chef for the DC 3 restaurant at the Santa Monica Airport. He is also co-owner (with my husband, Marvin Zeidler) of the successful Broadway Deli on the Promenade in Santa Monica. He and Marvin will soon open Capo, a contemporary Italian restaurant.

This chef is so creative, he draws on many cooking styles for influence. He claims French, Mexican, Italian, and American cuisines inspire him most. Extremely shy and modest, he is often called the most under-publicized chef in Los Angeles by colleagues and friends. Bruce is obsessed with good food, and unlike many chefs, often cooks and entertains at home.

on judy's kitchen: Bruce was a frequent guest on *Judy's Kitchen.* He prepared his healthful style of California cuisine on one program, and then followed that guest stint with demonstrations of sophisticated Mexican food. One show was taped at Rebecca's, which was designed by the internationally known architect Frank Gehry. It has a marine decor that makes patrons feel as if they're dining under water. We literally cooked our way around the restaurant. Bruce prepared the halibut cocktail at the seafood bar. Then we moved toward the open-fire rotisserie, where Bruce made chicken tacos and enchiladas. In another corner of the restaurant, we watched a cook making fresh tortillas.

I loved having Bruce demonstrate some of his special culinary techniques, like thin-slicing tuna and halibut for seviche. My greatest pleasure may have come from watching him demonstrate how to make an ancho chili sauce without searing your tonsils. Now that takes talent!

~ Peruvian-Style Tuna Seviche with Herb Oil

~ Halibut Cocktail

~ Chicken Tacos with Ancho Chili Sauce

~ Chicken Enchilada with Ancho Chili Sauce

~ Fruit Ices

a word about mexican-kosher

Mexican cuisine is great food for entertaining. Most of it can be prepared in advance in large quantities. It's easy on the budget, too, since it uses inexpensive ingredients like beans and rice, and small amounts of meat and poultry go a long way. Served with beer, margaritas, or sangria, a Mexican meal ensures a warm-hearted, relaxed party spirit for family and friends. This Latin theme also adds excitement to Sunday brunches, informal suppers, children's festivities, and all sorts of other lively occasions.

There is, however, one obvious drawback to Mexican food eaten outside of the home. Mexican cooking often uses lard, pork, and other non-kosher ingredients. It's safer, cheaper, and a lot more fun to make your own Mexican delicacies in your kosher kitchen.

peruvian-style tuna seviche with herb oil

In Mexico, pieces of assorted fish are marinated for hours to make seviche. At Rebecca's, Bruce uses the center cut of ahi tuna, and you can really taste the difference. You will never know this fish is raw: It looks white and firm; the acid in the lime juice actually cooks the ahi.

1   pound tuna, preferably ahi

Juice of 3 limes

2   tablespoons salt, or to taste

1   small red onion, sliced thinly into rounds

¼   cup chopped cilantro, for garnish

Tomato Salsa (recipe follows)

Herb Oil (recipe follows)

Slice the tuna into strips ⅛ inch thick and 2 inches long. Mix the lime juice and salt in a glass or stainless steel bowl. Add the tuna strips and marinate for 5 minutes.

To serve, spoon the salsa in the center of each plate and arrange the tuna slices fanned around the salsa. Generously brush the tuna with the Herb Oil, arrange onion slices, and sprinkle cilantro over the top.

Serves 6   Pareve

herb oil

2   garlic cloves

2   tablespoons fresh rosemary leaves

½   cup fresh Italian flat-leaf parsley leaves

2   tablespoons chopped fresh basil leaves

2   tablespoons fresh thyme leaves

2   tablespoons thinly sliced fresh chives

2   cups extra virgin olive oil

Salt and freshly ground black pepper, to taste

Combine the garlic, rosemary, parsley, basil, and thyme in a food processor and puree. Transfer to a heavy saucepan. Add the chives, olive oil, salt, and pepper, and warm over low heat. Serve at room temperature. (To store, cover with plastic wrap and refrigerate for up to 1 week.)

Makes about 2½ cups   Pareve

tomato salsa

2   tomatoes, peeled, seeded, and cut into ⅛-inch dice

½   medium white onion, cut into ⅛-inch dice

2   tablespoons minced cilantro

2   serrano chilies, seeded and minced

Salt, to taste

Toss the tomatoes, onion, cilantro, and serranos in a glass bowl and mix well. Season with salt. Cover with plastic wrap and refrigerate.

Makes about 1 cup   Pareve

halibut cocktail

On the sidewalks of Mexico, vendors sell fish cocktails in paper cups, made to order while you watch them prepare it. Bruce serves his halibut cocktail in wine glasses. Serve it with fresh tortilla chips or crackers.

Herb Oil (page 142)

1   pound halibut fillet

Juice of 3 limes

Salt, to taste

½   cup orange juice

4   tomatoes, peeled and seeded (see page 166)

1   tomato, fresh diced

1   onion, finely diced

1   avocado, peeled, pitted, and finely diced

2   serrano chilies, seeded, if desired, and finely diced

2   to 3 drops Tabasco sauce

2   tablespoons Sugar Syrup, or to taste (recipe follows)

Prepare the Herb Oil and let cool.

Slice the halibut into strips ⅛ inch thick and 2 inches long.

Mix the lime juice and salt in a glass or stainless steel bowl, add the halibut, and marinate for 3 minutes.

Heat the orange juice and the 4 tomatoes in a saucepan over medium heat to remove the raw tomato taste. Let cool. Place the tomato mixture in a blender or food processor and puree. Strain. You should have 1 cup.

In another glass or stainless steel bowl, combine the tomato puree, diced tomato, onion, avocado, serranos, Tabasco, and syrup. Drain the halibut, add to the mixture, and toss gently.

To serve, spoon the halibut cocktail into wine glasses and drizzle Herb Oil on top.

Serves 6 to 8   Pareve

sugar syrup

1   cup water

½   cup sugar

Bring the water and sugar to a boil in a saucepan and simmer for 2 minutes. Let cool. Pour into a wine bottle with a spout. Can be stored in refrigerator for as long as a month.

Makes 1 cup   Pareve

chicken tacos with ancho chili sauce

Corn tortillas are filled with a piquant chicken stew cooked in its own salsa, then the taco is topped with a sauce made from ancho chilies. Bruce describes a dried ancho chili as resembling a prune. When you plump or soak it in hot water or chicken stock, it becomes very meaty and turns a rich red color.

Ancho Chili Sauce (recipe follows)

2   tablespoons olive oil

1   large onion, chopped

2   boneless and skinless chicken breasts, cut into strips

2   serrano chilies, halved and sliced

3   tomatoes, peeled, seeded, and coarsely chopped (see page 166)

¼   cup Chicken Stock (page 167)

Salt, to taste

8   corn tortillas

1   cup shredded cabbage

1   avocado, peeled, pitted, and thinly sliced

Prepare the Ancho Chili Sauce and keep warm.

Heat the olive oil in a skillet over very high heat and sauté the onion until soft, about 5 minutes. Add the chicken and sauté until the chicken is tender and cooked through, about 5 minutes. Remove the chicken and keep warm. Add the serranos, tomatoes, and stock and simmer until the sauce is thick. Add the chicken and season with salt.

To serve, soften each tortilla by heating over the flame on top of the stove or in a tortilla warmer, turning until soft. Lay two of the tortillas, overlapping, on a work surface. Spoon the chicken stew on top. Top with cabbage, avocado, and a spoonful of Ancho Chili Sauce and roll up tight or serve open. Repeat with the remaining tortillas and filling.

To serve, place 2 tacos on each plate, and spoon additional Ancho Chili Sauce on top, spreading with the back of a spoon.

Serves 4   Meat

ancho chili sauce

4   dried ancho chilies, stemmed and seeded

1½   cups warm Chicken Stock (page 167) or hot water

1   tablespoon olive oil

¼   onion, diced

3   garlic cloves

Salt, to taste

Soak the chilies in stock to cover until soft, about 15 minutes.

Heat the olive oil in a skillet over medium heat and sauté the onion and garlic until soft. Place the chilies with the plumping liquid in a blender or food processor. Add the onion mixture and puree. The sauce should be thick and smooth. Pour additional liquid into the food processor while the motor is running if the sauce is too thick. Season with salt. Pour the sauce into a saucepan and keep warm.

Makes about 1½ cups   Meat

Note: If anchos or similar dried chilies are not readily available, substitute 1 roasted and peeled red bell pepper for each chili (see page 165 for roasting instructions) and ¼ teaspoon crushed red pepper when pureeing.

chicken enchilada with ancho chili sauce

Using the same Ancho Chili Sauce, Bruce created this chicken enchilada. When you slice the chicken breast very thin, it becomes more tender. In Mexico they usually heat tortillas in oil; Bruce finds it healthier and easier to soften them over a gas flame.

Ancho Chili Sauce (page 144)

2   large boneless and skinless chicken breasts

8   corn tortillas

1   avocado, peeled, pitted, and thinly sliced

2   tablespoons sesame seeds, toasted, for garnish

8   cilantro sprigs, for garnish

Prepare the Ancho Chili Sauce and keep warm.

Brown the chicken breasts on both sides in a skillet over medium-high heat. Cook until done. Thinly slice lengthwise. Heat the tortillas over an open flame, turning until soft, being careful not to burn them. Dip the tortilla in the sauce to soften. Place each tortilla on a work surface, and top with some chicken and avocado. Roll up tight.

To serve, place the enchiladas, seam side down, on plates and spoon the Ancho Chili Sauce on top, spreading with the back of the spoon to cover the tortilla. Garnish with toasted sesame seeds and cilantro.

Serves 4   Meat

fruit ices

banana-rum ice

Ices are cooling, refreshing and so easy to make. They are particularly welcome after a chili-laden dish. The Sugar Syrup keeps for several months in the refrigerator, so you can have it on hand for whenever you feel like making ices.

1   pound ripe bananas, peeled (4 or 5)

1⅓ cups cold Sugar Syrup (see page 168)

Juice of ½ lime or lemon, strained (2 tablespoons)

¾   cup noncarbonated mineral water

2   teaspoons white rum

Place the bananas in a blender or food processor and blend to a smooth puree. You should have about 2 cups. Mix the puree with the sugar syrup, lime juice, water, and rum in a large bowl. Freeze in an ice cream maker according to the manufacturer's instructions. Transfer to a plastic container and keep frozen until ready to serve.

Makes about 1 quart   Pareve

Note: If you do not have an ice cream maker, transfer the mixture to shallow metal pans and freeze until firm. Transfer to a food processor and process until smooth and fluffy. Serve immediately or return to the freezer until serving time.

lemon-lime ice

This tempting sweet-sour ice will satisfy any sweet craving and refresh the palate after Bruce's bold Mexican flavors.

•

½   cup strained fresh lemon juice

½   cup strained fresh lime juice

1½   cups noncarbonated mineral water

1¾   cups cold Sugar Syrup (see page 168)

Combine the lemon and lime juices, water, and syrup in a large bowl. Freeze in an ice cream maker according to the manufacturer's instructions. Transfer to a plastic container and keep frozen until ready to serve.

Makes about 1 quart   Pareve

papaya ice

A tropical treat with a smooth, creamy texture and a subtle flavor.

2   large ripe papayas, peeled and seeds discarded (about 1¾ pounds)

1½   cups Sugar Syrup (see page 168)

Juice of 1 lime, strained

Cut the papaya into chunks and place in a food processor. Blend to a smooth puree. You should have 2 cups of puree. Place the papaya puree in a large bowl and stir in the syrup and lime juice. Freeze in an ice cream maker according to the manufacturer's instructions. Transfer to a plastic container and keep frozen until ready to serve.

Makes about 3 cups   Pareve

strawberry ice

I am partial to this, especially when strawberries are in season, rich in color and bursting with flavor. Save a few perfect berries for garnish along with a sprig of mint.

2   pints fresh strawberries, washed and hulled

2   tablespoons strained fresh lime or lemon juice

2   cups Sugar Syrup (see page 168)

8   sliced strawberries for garnish

Mint, for garnish

Place the berries in a food processor and process to a smooth puree. You should have 3 ¼ cups of puree. Mix the puree, lime juice, and sugar syrup in a large bowl. Freeze in an ice cream maker according to the manufacturer's instructions. Transfer to a plastic container and keep frozen until ready to serve.

Makes about 1 quart   Pareve

chef's secrets

When fish is marinated in lime juice, it turns white and "cooks" quickly without heat, from the juice's acidic content.

Bruce makes his own sugar syrup and stores it in a wine bottle fitted with a pouring spout. It not only adds sweetness to sauces, it brings out their flavor.

KEN FRANK
an l.a. legend

about the chef: Most food professionals shake their heads with wonder when Ken Frank's name is mentioned. After all, at the tender age of twenty-one, Ken was head chef at La Guillotine restaurant in Los Angeles, where five years later he opened his own restaurant in the same space and named it La Toque. And we're not talking about a hamburger joint. La Toque became renowned nationwide for its exquisite French cuisine. At that time, an American chef—let alone such a young one—who cooked superb French food was an anomaly.

Now approaching forty, Ken reigns as the chef of Fenix restaurant in West Hollywood's Argyle hotel. An art deco masterpiece with an extraordinary view, Fenix combines classic French fare with contemporary California techniques and ingredients. This dining establishment is rated one of the city's best.

on judy's kitchen: Once the cameras began to roll, Ken looked fearless. No stagefright on his part. Ken is tall and thin, with intense eyes and a passion for perfection. His hands flew over the ingredients, yet he managed to make us all smile with his dry sense of humor. His Toasted Salmon Skin Salad and Duck Breast with Wild Mushrooms left me breathless, their flavor was so complex and their presentation so compelling. Yet both dishes proved relatively uncomplicated to make.

I was also impressed with Ken's soufflé technique. Timing a soufflé is downright tricky—even when you're not making one for television. Who wants the camera to close in on a rapidly sinking soufflé? Ken assured me he would deliver a perfect soufflé at just the right moment. He prepared four and placed one in the oven every five minutes. Thus, when the cue came to zoom in on the finished product, there was a tall and glorious soufflé. Wasn't I lucky to work with such a smart chef?

menu

~ Toasted Salmon Skin Salad

~ Duck Breast with Wild Mushrooms

~ Ken's Chocolate Espresso Soufflé

toasted salmon-skin salad

This Japanese-inspired salad is brilliant in concept as well as color. It has every taste sensation: a little sweet, a little sour, a little hot, a little spicy. There are Asian influences in many of Ken's dishes, and this one is a perfect example.

Olive oil, for pan

16 inches salmon skin (scaled)

3 cups radish sprouts

¼ cup julienned pink pickled ginger (see Note)

½ cup scrubbed and julienned Japanese cucumber

2 tablespoons salmon roe

Rice Wine Vinaigrette (recipe follows)

Preheat the broiler. Line a baking sheet with foil and brush with oil.

Lay the salmon skins on the baking sheet, skin side up. Place on the lowest rack and toast for 7 to 8 minutes, or until the skin is bubbly, brown, and crisp. Slice the salmon skin into ½-inch-wide strips. Set aside.

Toss the sprouts, pickled ginger, cucumber, and 1 tablespoon of the salmon roe in a large bowl. Set aside.

To serve, pour enough of the vinaigrette into the sprout mixture to moisten and toss lightly. Mound the salad on 4 plates and arrange the salmon skins on top like spokes of a wheel. Top with the remaining salmon roe.

Serves 4   Pareve

Note: Pickled ginger is available in Asian markets.

rice wine vinaigrette

1 teaspoon whole-grain mustard

2 tablespoons rice wine vinegar

Dash soy sauce

¼ cup sesame oil

Blend the mustard, vinegar, and soy sauce in a bowl. Using a wire whisk, blend in the oil. Cover with plastic wrap and refrigerate.

Makes ½ cup   Pareve

duck breast with wild mushrooms

Kosher ducks are easy to find in the freezer section of your kosher butcher shop or large supermarket. For this recipe, you need only the duck breasts. If you buy a whole duck, use the legs for duck chili or confit. Did you know that prior to World War II, the duck-goose liver industry in the Dordogne and Alsace regions of France was a major occupation of the local Jewish community?

2 duck breasts, trimmed of excess fat

Salt and freshly ground black pepper, to taste

2 tablespoons olive oil

½ pound chanterelles or other wild mushrooms in season, cleaned and sliced

½ pound oyster mushrooms, cleaned and sliced

2 shallots, minced

2 garlic cloves, minced

1 sprig tarragon, minced

Heat a large nonstick skillet over high heat. Season the duck breasts with salt and pepper and sauté, skin side down, until the skin is well browned and fat is rendered. Turn over and cook until medium-rare, 5 to 6 minutes. Let rest for 4 to 5 minutes.

Heat the olive oil in a large skillet over medium heat. Add the chanterelle and oyster mushrooms, season with salt and pepper, and sauté until golden brown, about 3 minutes. Add the shallots, garlic, and tarragon and sauté until the shallots and garlic are soft, about 3 minutes. Set aside and keep warm.

Remove the skin and slice each breast.

To serve, arrange the slices of duck, overlapping in a fan shape on large plates, and spoon mushrooms around the duck.

Serves 4   Meat

ken's chocolate espresso soufflé

This nondairy dessert is an impressive finale to any meal. The espresso intensifies the chocolate flavor. And just imagine, you can serve this soufflé with either a dairy or meat dinner!

Unsalted margarine, for coating the dishes

Granulated sugar, for coating the dishes

4   egg whites

3   tablespoons confectioners' sugar

3   egg yolks

¼   cup freshly brewed espresso, warm

6   ounces semisweet chocolate, melted and warm

Confectioners' sugar, for garnish

Preheat the oven to 400°F. Coat six ½-cup soufflé dishes evenly with margarine and dust with sugar. Set aside.

Whip the egg whites in a clean dry mixing bowl until frothy. Add the confectioners' sugar and continue beating until soft peaks form.

Combine the egg yolks, espresso, and chocolate in another bowl and mix well. Quickly fold the egg yolk mixture into the egg white mixture. Carefully pour the mixture into the soufflé dishes up to the rim without disturbing the sugar lining. Bake for 8 minutes, until cooked through and crisp on top.

To serve, sprinkle with confectioners' sugar and serve at once.

Serves 6   Pareve

chef's secrets

When skinning salmon for other recipes, save the skin (be sure to scale it first) with ⅛ inch of meat left on the skin, and freeze it for this salad.

The key to soufflé success is to coat the soufflé dishes evenly with butter or margarine and sugar. And when pouring the souffle mixture into the prepared dishes, do not disturb the butter and sugar.

about the chefs: The union of Nancy Silverton and Mark Peel is a marriage made in culinary heaven. She makes marvelous breads and pastries, and he's a brilliant chef. These two talents met when working at Spago on the Sunset strip. They fell in love, married, and have produced three beautiful children—and many, many wonderful meals.

Nancy began cooking in college, preparing vegetarian food for her dormitory. After apprenticing at a small Northern California restaurant, she attended the Cordon Bleu in London. Upon returning to Los Angeles, she became an assistant pastry chef at Michael's in Santa Monica. To continue her studies, Nancy enrolled at the famed École Le Nôtre outside Paris. Returning to Los Angeles, she became Spago's head pastry chef and developed some truly legendary desserts.

Mark began his career as a fry cook at a 24-hour coffee shop. While still in school, he started peeling vegetables for Wolfgang Puck at Ma Maison. As part of the apprenticeship, Mark worked in France at such Michelin three-star establishments as La Tour d'Argent in Paris and Le Moulin de Mougins in Provence. Later, he manned the kitchens at Michael's, Spago, and Chez Panisse in California. Mark and Nancy briefly worked together at New York's Maxwell's Plum.

In 1989, Nancy debuted La Brea Bakery to enthusiastic reviews. She is widely credited with being the first baker to introduce Mediterranean-inspired breads to Los Angeles. She and Mark opened Campanile, a California-Mediterranean restaurant, next door to La Brea Bakery in 1990. Campanile is consistently ranked one of the city's best.

Nancy has penned two great cookbooks, *Desserts* and *Nancy Silverton's Breads from La Brea Bakery*. She and Mark wrote a cookbook together, *Mark Peel & Nancy Silverton at Home*. The two are constant award winners: Nancy was named the 1990 Best Pastry Chef of the Year by the James Beard Foundation.

on judy's kitchen: Nancy's response to my invitation was really enthusiastic. She confided that Mark made the best chopped liver and brisket she had ever tasted, qualifying him as an almost-Jewish chef. Mark assured viewers that the chicken livers and the brisket he was preparing had been purchased at a kosher butcher shop. Nancy made fabulous panforte, a honey-fruit cake, which would be perfect to serve for Rosh Hashanah. I often make Mark's chopped liver for my Shabbat dinner, especially when the menu is Italian-inspired.

menu

~ Chopped Chicken Livers on Crostini

~ Braised Brisket with Beer

~ Panforte (Honey-Fruit Cake)

chopped chicken livers on crostini

Mark's Italian take on chopped chicken livers—with olive oil, sage, capers, and lemon—is an exciting change from the traditional schmaltz version. *Crostini* is Italian for thinly sliced and toasted bread rounds.

3   tablespoons olive oil

½   onion, finely chopped

1   pound chicken or duck livers, prepared according to kosher dietary laws

Salt and freshly ground black pepper, to taste

1   garlic clove, minced

Zest of 1 lemon

2   teaspoons minced fresh sage leaves

1   tablespoon capers, drained

1   teaspoon fresh lemon juice

¼   cup chopped parsley, for garnish

Thinly sliced and toasted bread rounds

Heat the oil in a large heavy skillet over medium heat and sauté the onion until soft, about 5 minutes. Sprinkle the livers with salt and pepper and add to the onion. Add the garlic and sauté, browning the livers on both sides.

Chop the lemon zest and sage together in a wooden chopping bowl or on a board. Spoon the warm liver mixture and the capers on top of the sage and lemon mixture and continue to chop until well blended. Mix in the lemon juice and season with salt and pepper. Transfer to a bowl, cover with plastic wrap, and refrigerate until ready to serve. To serve, sprinkle with parsley and serve with toasted bread rounds.

Serves 6   Meat

braised brisket with beer

This is Mark's famous braised brisket. Leftovers can be shredded for sandwiches. The beer adds a rich tangy flavor and a hint of hot peppers perks up the overall taste.

1   piece lean brisket (4½ pounds)

Kosher salt and freshly ground black pepper, to taste

1   tablespoon olive oil

2   large onions, cut into eighths

2   stalks celery, thinly sliced

2   carrots, cut into 2-inch chunks

½   cup parsley, stems only

¼   teaspoon crushed red pepper

2   sprigs thyme or ½ teaspoon dried thyme

3   garlic cloves, chopped

1   bay leaf

1   bottle (12 ounces) dark beer

1   cup Chicken Stock, or more to taste (see page 167)

1   tablespoon tomato paste

12 small red potatoes, scrubbed and steamed

8   ounces green beans, trimmed and steamed

Preheat the oven to 300°F.

Trim away any excess fat from the brisket. Rub it generously with salt and pepper. Brown the brisket on both sides in a heavy roasting pan over high heat for about 5 minutes. Remove the brisket and pour off all the fat. Place the onions, celery, and carrots in the pan, reduce the heat to medium, and scrape the bottom, adding liquid if needed to deglaze pan. Add the parsley stems, red pepper, thyme, garlic, bay leaf, beer, stock, tomato paste, salt, and pepper. Bring to a boil, return the meat to the roasting pan, cover, and bake for 2½ to 3 hours, or until tender. Skim off the fat.

Transfer the brisket to a heated platter and cut into thin slices across the grain. Remove and discard the bay leaf and thyme sprig. Transfer the vegetables to a food processor and blend. Push through a strainer onto the meat, adding more stock if the sauce is too thick. The mashed vegetables will thicken and flavor the sauce. Add the potatoes and green beans and reheat.

To serve, arrange the brisket slices on serving plates with potatoes, beans, and sauce.

Serves 8   Meat

panforte (honey-fruit cake)

This spicy, chewy Italian fruit and nut confection from Siena is a wonderful holiday treat. I love to serve it during Rosh Hashanah, instead of the traditional honey cake. Because the cake is so very dense and rich, you'll want to serve small slices.

1½   cups unbleached all-purpose flour

3   teaspoons unsweetened cocoa powder

¼   teaspoon ground cloves

¼   teaspoon ground nutmeg

½   teaspoon ground ginger

2   tablespoons ground cinnamon

1¼   cups hazelnuts, toasted and skinned (see page 165)

1   cup unblanched almonds, toasted (see page 165)

¾   cup chopped candied grapefruit peel

½   cup chopped dried apricots (see Note)

½   cup golden seedless raisins

8   dried figs, chopped (see Note)

¾   cup honey

1   cup sugar

Confectioners' sugar, for garnish

Preheat the oven to 300°F.

Combine the flour, cocoa powder, cloves, nutmeg, ginger, and cinnamon in a large bowl. Add the hazelnuts, almonds, grapefruit peel, apricots, raisins, and figs.

Combine the honey and sugar in a saucepan over high heat and bring to a boil. Cook until the mixture thickens, about 5 minutes. Add to the flour mixture, mixing with a wooden spoon until cool enough to handle. The dough will be very stiff. Mix with dampened hands, blending thoroughly.

Oil an 11-inch ring or spring form cake pan and place on a well-oiled, parchment-lined baking sheet. With wet hands, press the fruit mixture into the ring, spreading evenly. Bake for 1 hour, or until the edges look set and the top is slightly puffed. Let cool completely in the pan.

Run a knife around the edges of the mold or pan and remove the sides. Store at room temperature. Before serving, dust with confectioners' sugar and slice into thin wedges.

Makes 1 cake   Pareve

Note: If the fruit is dry and hard, pour on boiling water to cover and let soften, about 5 minutes. Drain before using.

Devoted to Desserts and Breads
part three

WHILE I GREW UP on traditional kosher desserts such as cheesecake, strudel, and mandelbrot, I now enjoy taking a more novel approach to sweets. Perhaps that's why I particularly appreciate the fresh approach taken by pastry chef Mary Bergin. ❧ Her Passover Apricot Macaroons add a creative twist to a classic recipe. Frankly, they taste much too good to bake just once a year. Her Pecan-Orange Shortcakes with Blueberry Compote combine two great fruit flavors and provide plenty of pleasing color for the eye. And you certainly don't have to keep kosher to fall in love with her Chocolate-Wrapped Hazelnut Cake! ❧ When most of us think of kosher breads, challah and rye bread are the first to come to mind, but master baker Tony Di Lembo's creations will quickly expand anyone's repertoire. His Crusty Rosemary Bread, rolls, and focaccia are a step away from addictive. ❧ Since these breads and desserts are dairy-free (except for the shortcake recipe) and olive oil is pareve, they can be paired with any of the appetizers and entrees in the first two sections of this book. Peruse the many options, but most of all, just get into the kitchen and bake. I promise that the results will be immensely satisfying, although with a little help from family and friends, they'll quickly disappear!

rich

MARY BERGIN
puckish pastry star

about the chef: A Hollywood landmark, Wolfgang Puck's Spago is one of America's most famous restaurants. And if you've ever ventured inside this celebrity-filled establishment, you surely encountered the extraordinary desserts of Mary Bergin. The executive pastry chef of Spago, Hollywood, from 1987 until 1992, and now at Spago Las Vegas, Mary has attracted enormous attention. Her recipes have appeared in numerous newspapers and national magazines, and she has co-authored her own cookbook, *Spago Desserts*, with Judy Gethers.

Mary continues to create new desserts for the Wolfgang Puck restaurant empire. The Caesar's Palace desert branch of Spago is a mecca for locals and tourists alike, and most would agree that Mary's desserts are a definite draw.

on judy's kitchen: Mary was a great guest. Not only do her warm smile and expressive eyes make her photogenic, she possesses a rare ability to make even a difficult dessert seem simple. Her skill and enthusiasm were so contagious that I was not at all surprised to learn that Mary's two children, Jackie and Anthony, share her passion for baking and love to experiment in the kitchen.

We taped the program's introduction at Spago. I felt like a star as the cameras followed me walking through the legendary restaurant to Mary's dazzling dessert display. The rest of the show was taped in a less star-studded setting—my home kitchen—but we had lots of fun baking together.

In keeping with her innovative style, Mary prepared two delicious Passover sweets: apricot macaroons and a three-layer hazelnut and walnut cake with a creamy chocolate filling. As a bonus, she whipped up some not-for-Passover, but definitely kosher, Pecan-Orange Shortcakes.

menu

~ Passover Apricot Macaroons

~ Chocolate-Wrapped Hazelnut Cake

~ Pecan-Orange Shortcakes with Blueberry Compote

These macaroons were originally created for the Passover seder that is held at Spago restaurant. Mary calls them Little Haystacks. When I watched Mary bake these on *Judy's Kitchen*, I couldn't wait to try the recipe, which has now become a Passover favorite in my family.

½	cup (tightly packed) dried apricots, cut into quarters
¾	cup plus 1 tablespoon sugar
4	egg whites
4½	cups unsweetened shredded coconut (see Note)

Preheat the oven to 350°F. Line baking sheets with parchment paper.

Combine the apricots, ½ cup water, and 1 tablespoon of the sugar in a medium saucepan over medium heat. Poach until tender and only about 1 tablespoon of water remains, about 10 minutes. Cool slightly.

Transfer to a food processor, add the remaining ¾ cup sugar, the egg whites, and ½ cup of the coconut, and process until the apricots are pureed. Start with on/off pulses, then let the machine run. Transfer to the large bowl of an electric mixer fitted with the paddle attachment or beaters and add the remaining 4 cups coconut. On medium speed, beat until the coconut is well blended. Stop the machine and check the texture—the mixture should hold together when pinched. Continue mixing, if necessary.

Divide the dough into 24 equal portions. With lightly moistened fingers, shape each portion first into rounds and then into pointed cone shapes, resembling haystacks. Arrange on baking sheets, 1 inch apart. Bake for 15 to 20 minutes, or until the tops are

well browned. Cool on a rack and store in an airtight container.

Makes 2 dozen macaroons   Pareve

Note: If using sweetened coconut, reduce the sugar by ¼ cup.

This elegant three-layer cake is wrapped in a chocolate band and garnished with chopped hazelnuts for a dramatic effect. Since no flour is used, the cake is an ideal choice for a Passover menu.

	Unsalted margarine, for cake pans
3	tablespoons unsweetened cocoa powder
1	cup hazelnuts, toasted (see page 165)
1	cup walnuts, toasted (see page 165)
1	cup sugar
6	eggs, separated
	Creamy Chocolate Filling (recipe follows)
	Chocolate Band (recipe follows)
¼	cup chopped toasted hazelnuts, for garnish

Preheat the oven to 350°F.

Butter three 9-inch cake pans, dust lightly with 1 tablespoon of the cocoa, and place on baking sheets. Set aside.

Place the hazelnuts, walnuts, remaining 2 tablespoons cocoa, and ¼ cup of the sugar in a food processor and process until finely ground. Set aside.

Combine the egg yolks and ½ cup of the sugar in the bowl of an electric mixer. Beat until

Dry Storage: 928 - 3566

thick and pale yellow. Transfer to a large mixing bowl. In another clean electric mixer bowl, beat the egg whites until soft peaks form. With the machine running, gradually pour in the remaining ¼ cup sugar and continue beating until stiff but not dry. Stir half of the nut mixture into the egg yolk mixture. Fold in the remaining nut mixture with one third of the egg whites. Fold in the remaining egg whites. Spoon the mixture into the 3 prepared pans.

Bake for 40 to 45 minutes, or until a toothpick inserted in the center of each layer comes out clean and the layers shrink away from the sides of the pans. Invert onto racks, but do not remove from the pans until cool.

Prepare the Creamy Chocolate Filling.

Turn the pans right side up and run a sharp knife around cakes to loosen. Place 1 cake round on a large platter and spread with filling, place a second round on top and spread with filling, top with third round and spread with filling. Cover with plastic wrap and refrigerate for 1 hour, or until firm.

Prepare the Chocolate Band.

Remove the cake from the refrigerator. Pick up the Chocolate Band and carefully wrap it around the cake, pinching the ends together and cutting off the excess tail with sharp scissors. Refrigerate the cake until the band is set, about 30 minutes. Carefully peel off the wax paper. Sprinkle chopped nuts on top of cake. Refrigerate until ready to serve.

Makes one 3-layer cake   Pareve

creamy chocolate filling

4	ounces semisweet chocolate, broken into pieces
½	pound (2 sticks) unsalted margarine
½	teaspoon vanilla extract
2	tablespoons coffee
2	egg yolks

Melt the chocolate in the top of a double boiler over hot water on moderate heat, stirring until smooth.

Cream the margarine in the bowl of electric mixer. Beat in the vanilla, coffee, and melted chocolate. Add the egg yolks, one at a time, beating well after each addition. Beat at high speed for 1 or 2 minutes, until the color lightens to a pale caramel shade and the mixture is very smooth and light.

Makes about 2 cups   Pareve

chocolate band

6	ounces semisweet chocolate, melted

Place a large sheet of wax paper on a work area. Make a band of wax paper to the height and a little longer than the circumference of the cake. Spread melted chocolate evenly over the wax paper, ⅛ inch thick. Let set for 5 minutes, or until the chocolate is no longer shiny but is still pliable.

Makes 1 chocolate band   Pareve

pecan-orange shortcakes with blueberry compote

The shortcakes are definitely not for Passover, but the blueberry compote can be served with the macaroons and/or a fruit sorbet.

2¾ cups all-purpose flour

1 tablespoon plus 1 teaspoon baking powder

⅓ cup sugar

1 teaspoon ground cinnamon

1 teaspoon salt

1¼ cups chopped pecans, toasted (see page 165)

1 tablespoon grated orange zest

10 tablespoons unsalted cold butter, cut into pieces

1 cup heavy cream

1 teaspoon ground cinnamon mixed with 1 tablespoon sugar

1 cup heavy cream, whipped, for garnish

Blueberry Compote (recipe follows)

Preheat the oven to 350°F. Butter a baking sheet.

Combine the flour, baking powder, sugar, cinnamon, and salt in a food processor and blend. Add the pecans and orange zest and blend. Add the butter and blend until the mixture resembles meal or crumbs. With the motor running, pour in cream and process until the mixture forms a ball. Do not overprocess.

Turn the dough out onto a floured surface and knead it into a flat disk about 1 inch thick. Cut into twelve 2-inch rounds with a cookie cutter. Place on the baking sheet, 2 inches apart. Bake for 20 to 25 minutes, or until golden brown. Cool and sprinkle with cinnamon-sugar.

To serve, cut each shortcake in half horizontally and place on a serving plate. Spoon a generous dollop of whipped cream on the bottom half and top with a spoonful of Blueberry Compote. Cover with top half of shortcake and remaining compote.

Serves 12   Dairy

blueberry compote

2 pints blueberries, or other berries in season

1 vanilla bean, split in half, seeds removed

1 cinnamon stick

¾ cup sugar

2 tablespoons fresh lemon juice

Combine the blueberries, vanilla bean, cinnamon stick, sugar, and lemon juice in a saucepan over medium heat and bring to a boil. Reduce the heat and simmer for 15 minutes, or until thick and shiny. Let cool.

Makes about 2 cups   Pareve

chef's secrets

❧ Always use a clean, dry whisk and bowl when beating egg whites. Start on low speed until the whites lose their yellow color.

❧ Unlike most macaroon recipes, this one does not call for stiffly beaten egg whites. By incorporating the whites into the other ingredients, the macaroons are quicker and easier to prepare. In addition, the batter may be frozen, and the macaroons baked when needed.

❧ Placing cake pans on baking sheets helps the layers bake more evenly.

about the chefs: Karen Salk and Tony Di Lembo have created a winning partnership. Together they run Breadworks, a Los Angeles wholesale bakery, which has grown to include three retail stores in Los Angeles, Santa Monica, and Hancock Park. Tony serves as head chef, while Karen manages the business end of the operation.

Karen obtained a degree in finance from the University of Southern California and has considerable restaurant management experience. Tony earned a bachelor's degree in business management and Italian from the University of Pittsburgh before graduating with honors from the prestigious Culinary Institute of America in Hyde Park, New York. To further his education, he also worked in Italy and France for several years.

Tony was the personal chef for Barbra Streisand for two years and then worked in Los Angeles restaurant kitchens before teaming up with Karen. Together, they opened Indigo restaurant. The eclectic eatery quickly became a favorite of Angelenos, who fell for the quirky cuisine and the innovative breads. When the pair opened Breadworks, they decided to sell the restaurant and focus solely on the bakery. Seeing the outstanding success they've achieved, it was clearly a smart decision.

on judy's kitchen: When I first called Karen and Tony and asked them to appear on my television show, their response was a gracious, "Thanks, but no thanks." Since they had never appeared on television, they were concerned. But I didn't give up, and eventually they agreed to be guests.

You never would have known that they were rookies. Karen opened the program by talking about Breadworks and displaying an array of their breads, rolls, muffins, and scones. Tony took over and clearly explained the sometimes mysterious techniques of bread making. I think viewers were pleased that they could learn how to make one basic recipe and transform it into three distinctive breads.

menu

~ Crusty Rosemary Bread

~ Crusty Rosemary Rolls

~ Rosemary, Onion, and Garlic Focaccia

Once you've mastered this recipe and made your first loaf of bread, double the recipe and bake rosemary rolls and rosemary focaccia (recipe follows). Store bread in a plastic bag in the freezer, then heat and serve. No one will guess it wasn't baked that morning.

Malt syrup is a dough enhancer. It is not essential to the recipe but helps produce a better-looking loaf that lasts longer than one made without it. It is available in most health food stores.

Rosemary Bread Dough

½   small onion, diced

3   garlic cloves

⅓   cup rosemary

1   cup warm water

1   envelope dry yeast or 1 cake compressed yeast (0.6 ounces)

2   tablespoons olive oil

1   teaspoon malt syrup (optional)

1   teaspoon salt

3½   to 4 cups bread flour or unbleached all-purpose flour

Olive oil

Flour, for dusting

Place the onion, garlic, and rosemary in a food processor or blender and blend, adding ½ cup of the water in a thin stream, until well blended. Set aside.

Dissolve the yeast in the remaining ½ cup of warm water until foamy, about 1 minute. Pour the yeast mixture into the large bowl of a heavy-duty electric mixer fitted with the dough hook attachment. Blend in the onion mixture. Add the olive oil, malt (if using), and salt. Add 2½ cups of the flour and beat on medium speed. When the flour is combined, turn the mixer to slow and knead for about 10 minutes, adding an additional cup of flour as necessary to prevent the dough from sticking to the bowl. Dough should be very firm. Occasionally redistribute the dough in the bowl, if necessary.

Brush a large bowl with olive oil, oil the dough lightly, place in the bowl and cover loosely with plastic wrap. Allow to rise in a warm draftfree place until double in bulk, about 1 hour.

Turn the dough out onto a floured board and knead for 1 minute. Cut into 2 equal pieces and dust each with flour. Form each round by turning dough inside itself with your fingertips, stretching down the sides and tucking underneath loaf. Dip your fingers in flour as necessary to prevent sticking. Roll in flour, place on 4-inch squares of parchment paper, cover with a towel, and let rise in a warm draftfree place until double in bulk, about 45 minutes.

Place a pizza stone in the oven and preheat to 450°F.

Slash loaves once across the center with a razor or sharp knife, cutting about ½ inch deep. If you slash like this, the loaf will open up, creating 2 round loaves attached in the center.

Place the bread, with the square of parchment paper, on the stone and bake for 30 minutes, or until the loaves are brown and sound hollow when tapped on the bottom.

Makes 2 loaves   Pareve

crusty rosemary rolls

Rosemary Bread Dough, prepared through the first rise (page 162)

¼ cup olive oil

Preheat the oven to 400°F. Oil a foil-lined baking sheet or place a pizza stone in the oven, if using.

Tear off large pieces of dough about the size of a lemon (about 2½ ounces each). With well-floured fingertips, shape each piece of dough into a small round. Place on the baking sheet or pizza stone, 2 inches apart. Bake for 15 to 20 minutes, or until golden brown. Serve hot.

Makes about 20 rolls   Pareve

rosemary, onion, and garlic focaccia

The dough has a certain amount of elasticity; the margarine on the jelly-roll pan helps prevent it from shrinking from the edges of the pan.

Rosemary Bread Dough, prepared through the first rise (page 162)

Margarine or Crisco, for pan

1 small onion, sliced lengthwise

4 garlic cloves, chopped

½ cup fresh rosemary

Kosher salt and freshly ground black pepper, to taste

¼ cup olive oil

Divide the dough in half.

Preheat the oven to 425°F.

Brush a jelly-roll pan with margarine or Crisco. Flatten the dough in the pan and stretch and press it out with your hands to cover as much of the bottom as possible. The dough will be sticky and may not entirely cover the bottom of the pan. Cover the dough with a towel and let it relax for 10 minutes, then stretch it again until it reaches the edges of the pan.

Sprinkle the top of the focaccia with the onions, garlic, rosemary, salt, and pepper. Drizzle the oil over the top. (To prepare the dough in advance, cover with plastic wrap and refrigerate.) Let rise for 15 minutes or until double. Place on the lower rack of the oven and bake for 15 minutes or until golden brown. Serve hot or warm.

Serves 10 to 12   Pareve

chef's secrets

❧ Use fresh herbs whenever possible; they are more aromatic than dried herbs. They also add attractive color to the baked loaves.

❧ A scale is an essential part of the baker's kitchen equipment. It makes it possible to achieve uniformity in baking rolls, breads, and pastries.

❧ When baking bread, lay the loaves directly on a hot surface. In a conventional oven, you will obtain the best results from baking bread on a special pizza stone, unglazed quarry tiles, or even on a preheated metal baking sheet.

❧ Score bread across the top of the loaf, cutting ½ inch deep, just before baking.

kitchen tips

clarifying butter

The process of clarifying butter removes the milk solids and most of the water from the butter. Clarified butter can be used for sautéing at high temperatures, when whole butter would burn. Do at least half a pound of unsalted butter at a time. It keeps forever.

Place the butter in a saucepan over low heat and simmer for 5 minutes, or until the milk solids have separated and the butter is clear. Remove from the heat and allow the solids to settle to the bottom. Strain through a fine-mesh strainer, stopping as soon as any milky residue appears in the clear stream of butter. Or refrigerate until the butter hardens, then poke a hole in the butter and pour out and discard the milky residue. Refrigerate or freeze.

making crème fraîche

Crème fraîche is a thick cultured cream with a nutty flavor. It's sold in the dairy sections of many super-markets and gourmet shops, but it's also very easy to make at home—and much less expensive.

Heat 1 cup heavy cream in a saucepan over low heat to lukewarm (95° to 100°F). Whisk in 2 table-spoons buttermilk. Pour into a jar, cover with plastic wrap, and let sit at room temperature for 24 to 36 hours. The mixture will become thick and flavorful. Refrigerate. (Crème fraîche will keep for up to 1 week in the refrigerator.)

roasting garlic

Roasting garlic mellows its flavor and softens the garlic to a spreadable puree that's great on crusty bread or focaccia or added to mashed potatoes. Our family favorite is to mix roasted garlic puree with softened butter or margarine, spread on half a bagel and broil until golden brown and bubbly. Delicious!

Preheat the oven to 350°F. Line a baking sheet with foil. Cut heads of garlic in half and place, cut side up, on the baking sheet. Pour 1 tablespoon olive oil over each half head of garlic. Sprinkle with 3 to 4 tablespoons of water, cover tightly with the foil, and bake for 30 to 40 minutes. Open the foil and bake for 5 to 7 minutes more, or until the garlic is golden brown. Remove from the oven and cool. Squeeze the softened garlic into a food processor or blender, discarding the skin. Add just enough olive oil to make pureeing possible.

toasting nuts

Preheat the oven to 350°F. Line a baking sheet with foil. To toast walnuts, pecans, or almonds, arrange the nuts in a single layer on the baking sheet. Bake for 5 minutes, turning and shaking frequently until the nuts are evenly brown. Watch carefully, as they burn easily. To toast hazelnuts, spread a single layer of nuts on the baking sheet and bake, turning and shaking the pan frequently, until the nuts are evenly browned, 10 to 15 minutes. Watch carefully, as they burn easily. Place nuts in a soft towel and rub gently until most of the skins fall off.

To keep nuts fresh, store in plastic bags in the freezer. Toast them before using to enhance their flavor and bring back their crunchy texture. Substitute ground nuts for some of the flour in your favorite cake, pie crust, or bread recipe, or sprinkle them in buttered cake pans before pouring in the batter, to keep the cake from sticking to the pan.

roasting peppers

Patrick Healy's technique for roasting peppers (see page 105) imparts a smoky flavor. The following way is easy and foolproof, a good choice for when you don't want the peppers to have a smoky taste.

Preheat the oven to 375°F. Place a large sheet of foil over the lower rack of the oven. Place the peppers or chilies on the middle or top rack of the oven. Bake for 20 to 30 minutes, or until the skin has puffed and darkened slightly on top. Turn each pepper over and continue to bake for 10 to 15 minutes more. Remove from the oven, and while the peppers are still warm, very carefully peel off the skins, reserving the juices. Pull out the stems and discard the seeds. Cut the peppers into segments that follow their natural ridges. Use as directed in the recipe or layer the peppers in a bowl with the juices and enough olive oil to cover. Cover with plastic wrap and refrigerate.

reducing sauces

A simple secret to enhancing sauces, soups, and stews is to simmer or boil the liquid until it reduces in volume and the flavors intensify. It's amazing how rich a sauce, soup, or stew can become without the addition of cream or butter.

peeling tomatoes

Using a sharp knife, cut a shallow X in the skin at the bottom of each tomato. Drop the tomatoes, two or three at a time into boiling water, count to 10, then lift them out with a slotted spoon and plunge them into a bowl filled with ice water. Peel the tomatoes, and they are ready to be used in any recipe you like. To seed the tomatoes, cut them in half and gently squeeze the juice and seeds out of each half, reserving them for a sauce. Chop or dice the flesh as directed in the recipe.

making kosher balsamic-style vinegar

Balsamic vinegar is made with red wine vinegar aged in barrels, sometimes up to twenty-four years. I have been flooded with requests for a kosher version. Since it's difficult to find such a vinegar, I decided to learn how to make a substitute that duplicates balsamic vinegar's distinctive flavor.

Combine 1 cup red wine vinegar and 1½ cups kosher concord grape wine in a heavy saucepan over high heat and bring to a boil. Reduce the heat and simmer until reduced to ½ cup, about 20 minutes. Cool and store in a sterilized jar.

making homemade stock

The art of making stock is a useful one for the kosher cook, since it is the safest way of knowing exactly what ingredients go into its preparation. Stock is the perfect base for soups, sauces, or stews.

Stock is a liquid base enhanced with vegetables, fish, meat, chicken, or turkey and slowly cooked until the flavors intensify. A stock can simmer anywhere from thirty minutes to five hours. Stocks can be refrigerated in covered containers for up to three days or frozen for several months.

vegetable stock

¼   cup olive oil

4   onions, chopped

4   carrots, chopped

2   parsnips, chopped

4   stalks celery, chopped

3   leeks, white and green parts, chopped

3   bay leaves

4   garlic cloves, crushed

6   sprigs fresh thyme or 2 teaspoons dried thyme

½   cup chopped parsley

8   peppercorns

2   tablespoons soy sauce (optional)

Salt, to taste

Heat the oil in a large stockpot over medium heat and sauté the onions, carrots, parsnips, celery, and leeks until soft and lightly browned, about 5 minutes. Stir in the bay leaves, garlic, thyme, parsley, peppercorns, soy sauce (if using), and a pinch of salt. Add 3 quarts water and bring to a boil. Reduce the heat and simmer, partially covered, for 2 hours. Season with salt to taste. Remove from heat, strain, pressing as much liquid as possible from the vegetables, then discard them. Let cool. Pour into containers, cover, and refrigerate or freeze until needed.

Makes about 8 cups

chicken stock

8   pounds chicken parts (necks, backs, carcasses, thighs), cut into pieces

3   onions, quartered

4   carrots, cut into 1-inch pieces

4   stalks celery, cut into 1-inch pieces

2   leeks, coarsely chopped

3   sprigs parsley

2   bay leaves

2   garlic cloves, crushed

6   peppercorns

1½   teaspoons salt, or to taste

Combine the chicken, onions, carrots, celery, leeks, parsley, bay leaves, garlic, peppercorns, and salt in a large stockpot or saucepan. Add cold water to cover, about 4 quarts, and bring to a boil over medium-high heat. Reduce heat and simmer, partially covered, for 2 to 3 hours, or until the stock has developed a good flavor. Spoon off any foam that rises to the top during the cooking. If the water cooks down below the level of the ingredients, add more water and season with salt to taste.

Remove from heat and strain through a fine-mesh strainer. Discard the vegetables and save the chicken for other use. Remove the grease from the stock before using. The easiest way to degrease the stock is to refrigerate it for several hours; the grease will solidify on top and can be easily removed with a spoon. (Stock may be kept for 2 or 3 days in the refrigerator or it can be frozen.)

Makes about 6 cups

fish stock

3   pounds fish and bones from any nonoily kosher fish

2   onions, thinly sliced

2   carrots, cut into 1-inch pieces

1   stalk celery, cut into 1-inch pieces

1   garlic clove, crushed

Herb bouquet, including bay leaf, fennel seeds, peppercorns, parsley, and thyme, tied in a piece of cheesecloth

1   cup dry white wine

Salt, to taste

Place the fish, onions, carrots, celery, garlic, herb bouquet, and wine in a large stockpot. Add wine and cold water to cover and bring to a boil. Reduce the heat and simmer, partially covered, for 45 minutes. Remove the herb bouquet. Pour the broth through a strainer lined with cheesecloth and cool. Use as required or pour into containers, cover, and refrigerate or freeze until needed.

Makes about 2 cups

pareve chicken stock

Pareve Chicken Stock is a commercial powdered chicken-flavored base that contains no meat or dairy products. It may be used in recipes for both dairy and meat meals. You can find it in most supermarkets in the kosher food department.

To reconstitute this powdered base, dissolve 1 tablespoon per cup of hot water and you have an instant pareve chicken-flavored stock.

to use kosher meat casings

To use liquid-packed casings, soak in warm water for 15 to 30 minutes, and flush by attaching casing to a water faucet and running warm water through. To use salt-packed casings, increase soaking time to 1 to 2 hours, or until soft and flexible.

Outfit an electric grinder or a sausage maker, either hand-cranked or electric, with a special sausage attachment. Pour or feed the mixture into the feeder of the machine.

Slide a prepared sausage casing onto the attachment and tie the end. Start grinding to partly fill the casing. To shape the first sausage length, simply twist the sausage casing about 4 to 5 inches from the tied end of the casing. Continue filling and twisting the casings at 4- to 5-inch intervals. As you work, always twist the casing in alternate directions.

After a yard or so of sausages has been filled and twisted, cut off the sausage casing and tie the end. Continue preparing sausages until all the fill-

ing has been used. If you find any air bubbles, use a needle to prick the casings at the point where the bubbles occur.

Note: I have been fortunate in obtaining kosher casings from my butcher, but plastic wrap works just as well (see page 135).

sugar syrup

2   cups cold water

2½   cups sugar

Combine the water and sugar in a large saucepan over medium heat and cook, stirring with a wooden spoon, only until the sugar has dissolved. When the syrup comes to a full boil, remove the saucepan from the heat immediately and let cool. Pour the syrup into a large jar, cover, and refrigerate.

Makes 3½ cups

TABLE OF EQUIVALENTS

The exact equivalents in the following tables have been rounded for convenience.

LIQUID AND DRY MEASURES

U.S.		METRIC	
¼	teaspoon	1.25	milliliters
½	teaspoon	2.5	milliliters
1	teaspoon	5	milliliters
1	tablespoon (3 teaspoons)	15	milliliters
1	fluid ounce (2 tablespoons)	30	milliliters
¼	cup	60	milliliters
⅓	cup	80	milliliters
1	cup	240	milliliters
1	pint (2 cups)	480	milliliters
1	quart (4 cups, 32 ounces)	960	milliliters
1	gallon (4 quarts)	3.84	liters
1	ounce (by weight)	28	grams
1	pound	454	grams
2.2	pounds	1	kilogram

OVEN TEMPERATURES

FAHRENHEIT	CELSIUS	GAS
250	120	½
275	140	1
300	150	2
325	160	3
350	180	4
375	190	5
400	200	6
425	220	7
450	230	8
475	240	9
500	260	10

LENGTH MEASURES

U.S.		METRIC	
⅛	inch	3	millimeters
¼	inch	6	millimeters
½	inch	12	millimeters
1	inch	2.5	centimeters

spaghettini with watercress aglio e olio

border grill skewered salmon

chicken breasts with prune stuffing

passover apricot macaroons

sauteéd shiitake mushrooms

beef goulash

mixed berry gratin